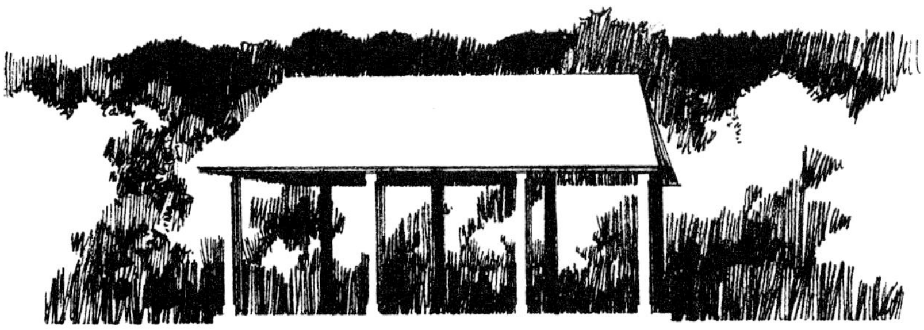

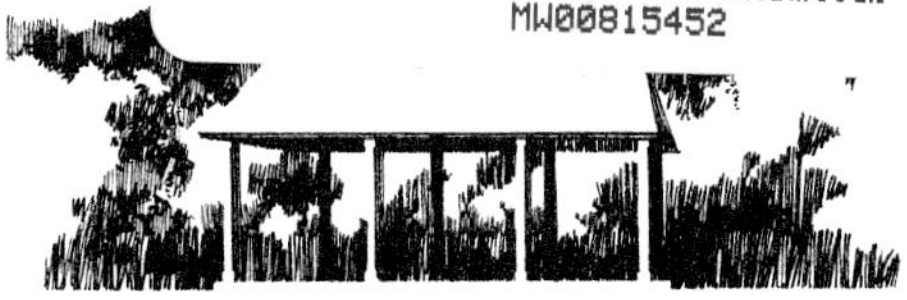

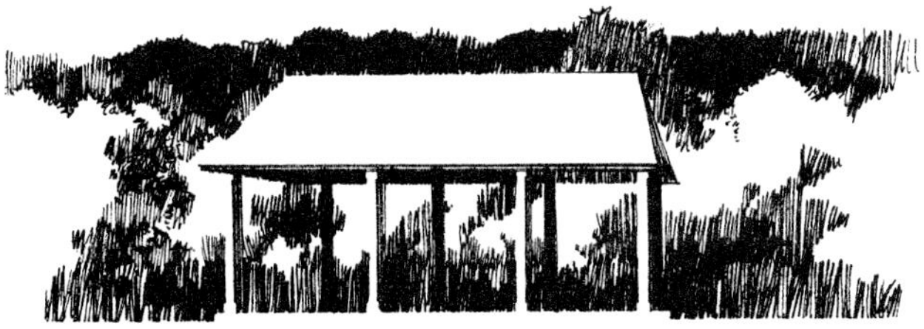

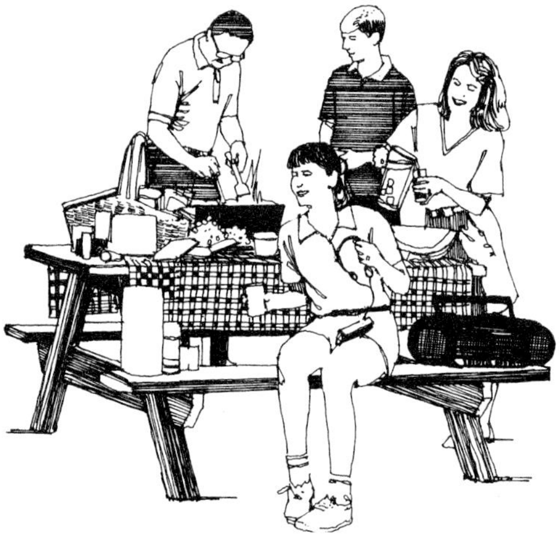

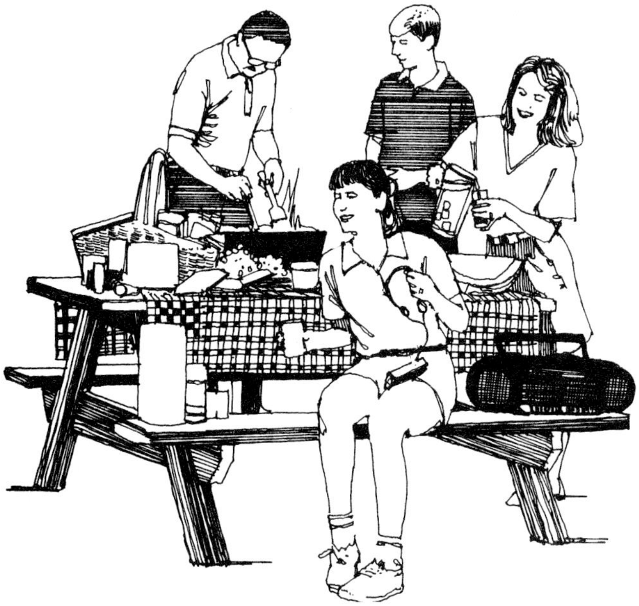

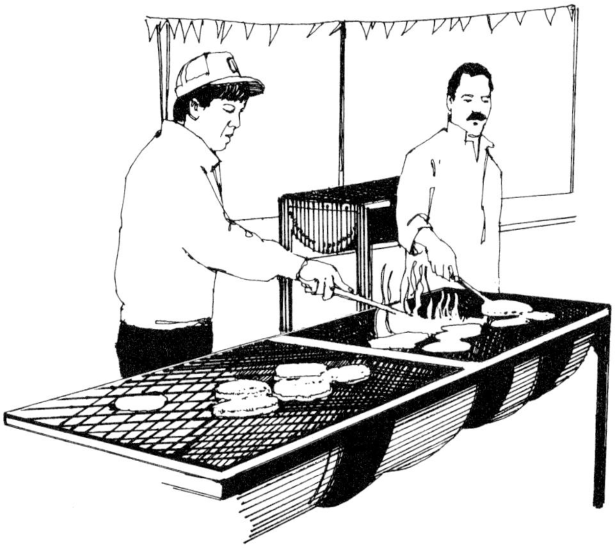

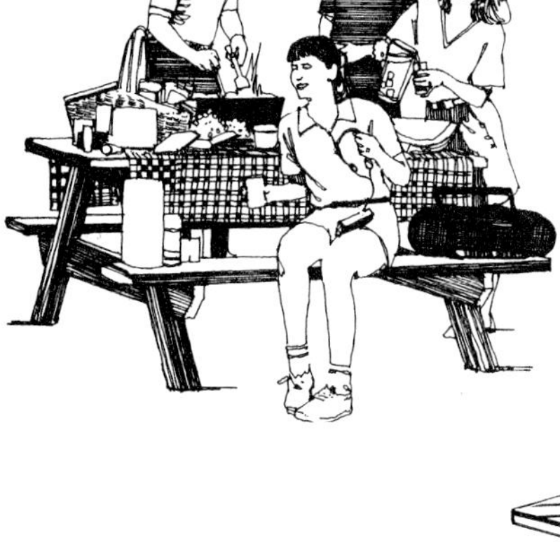

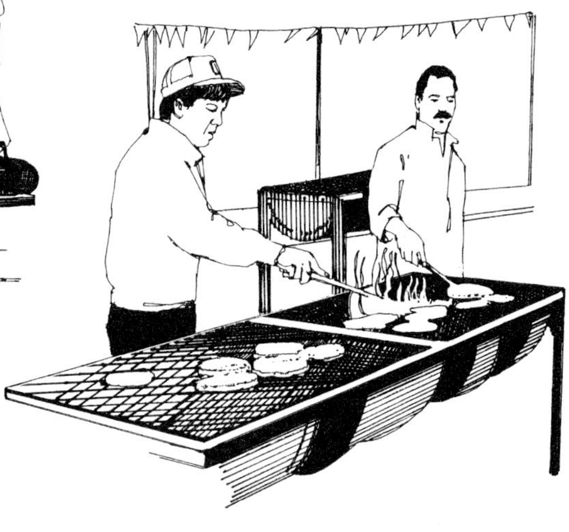

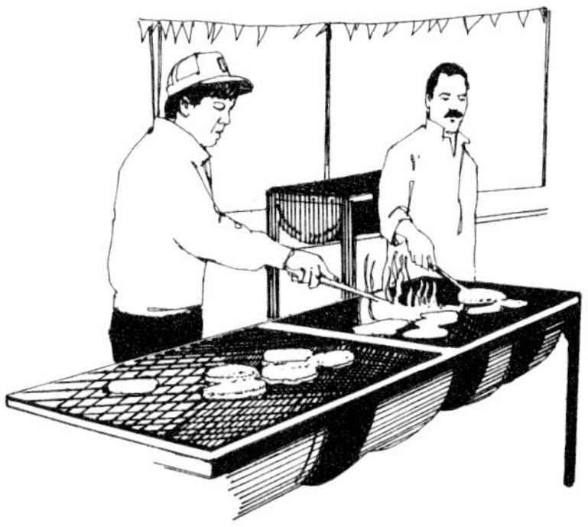

■ Picnic

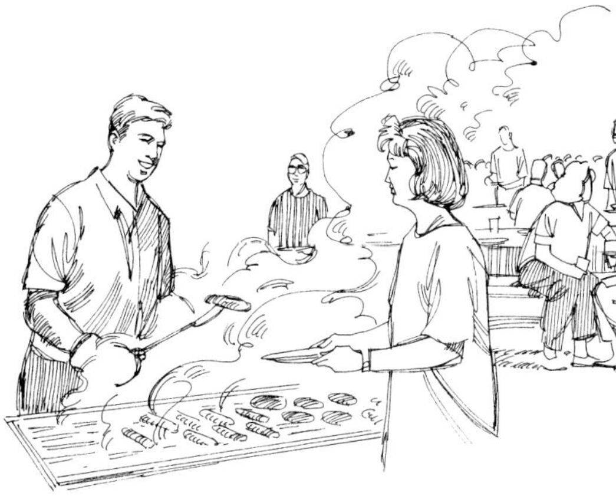

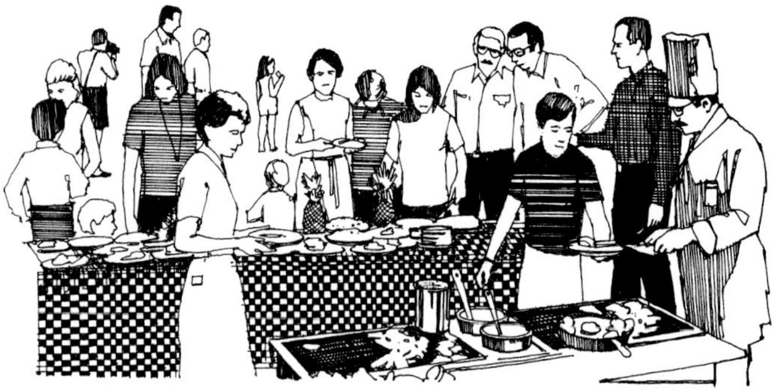

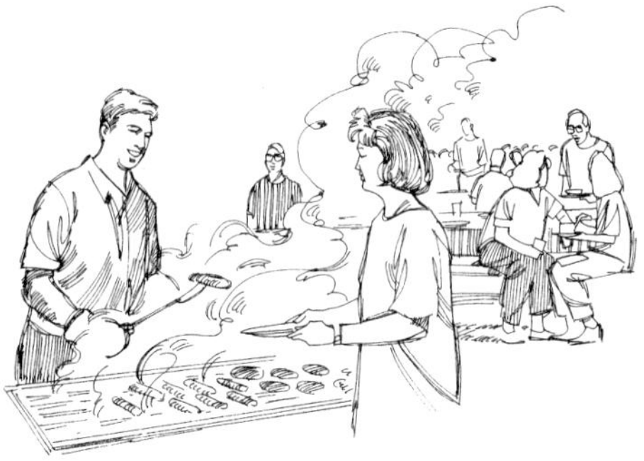

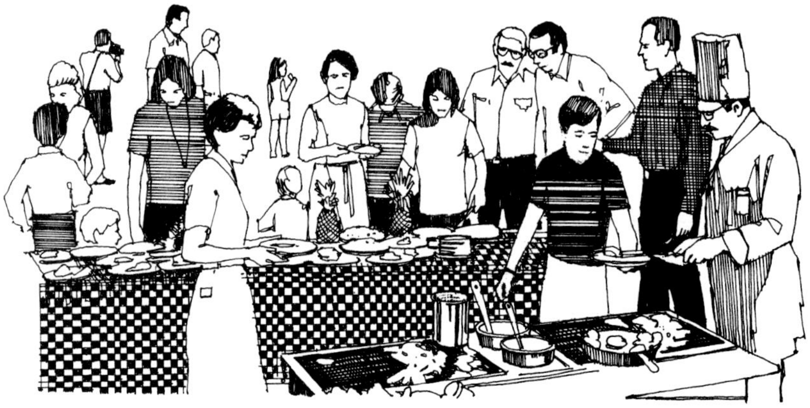

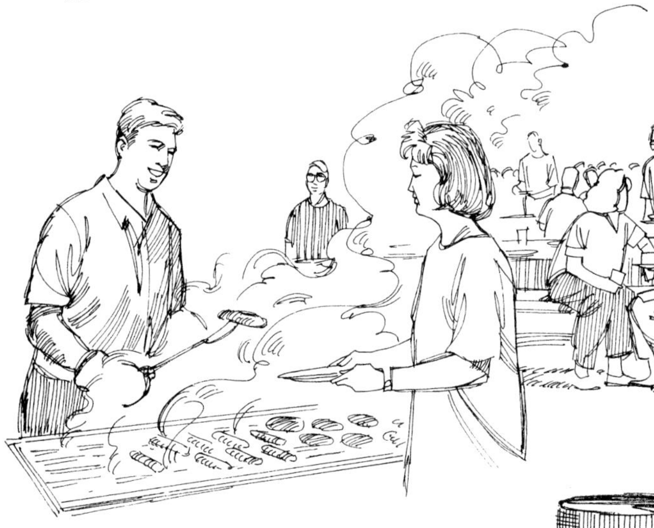

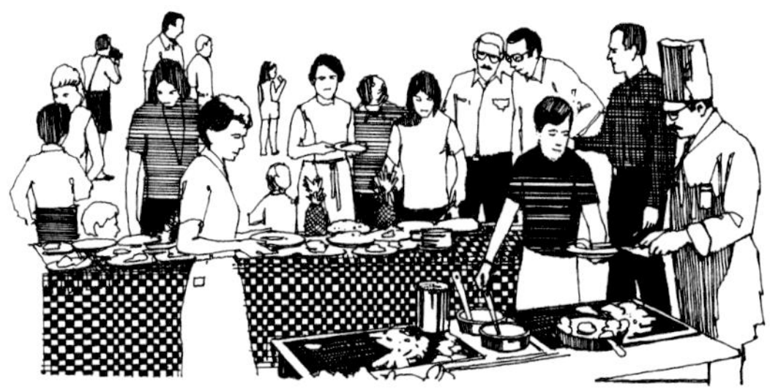

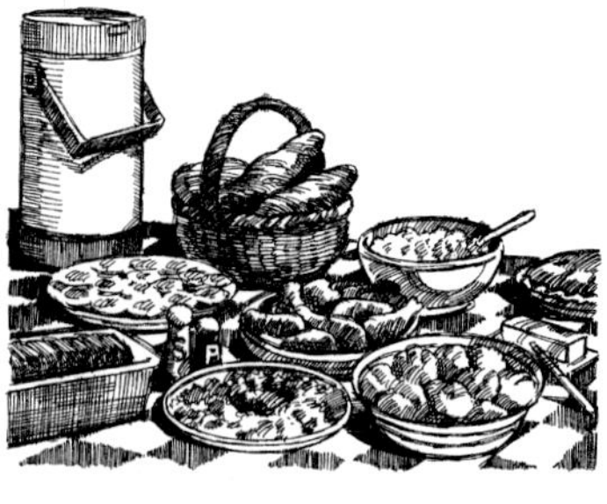

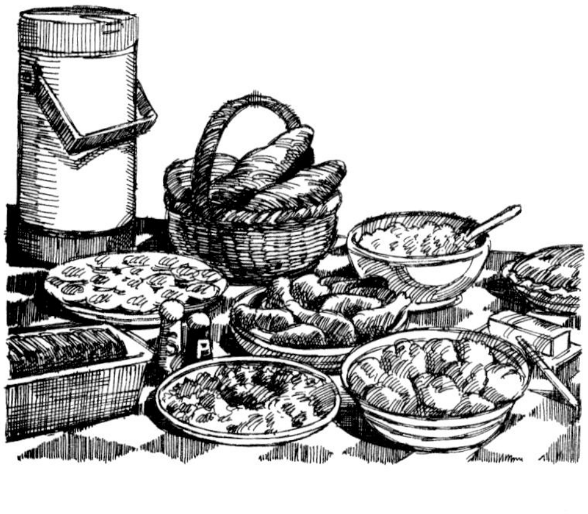

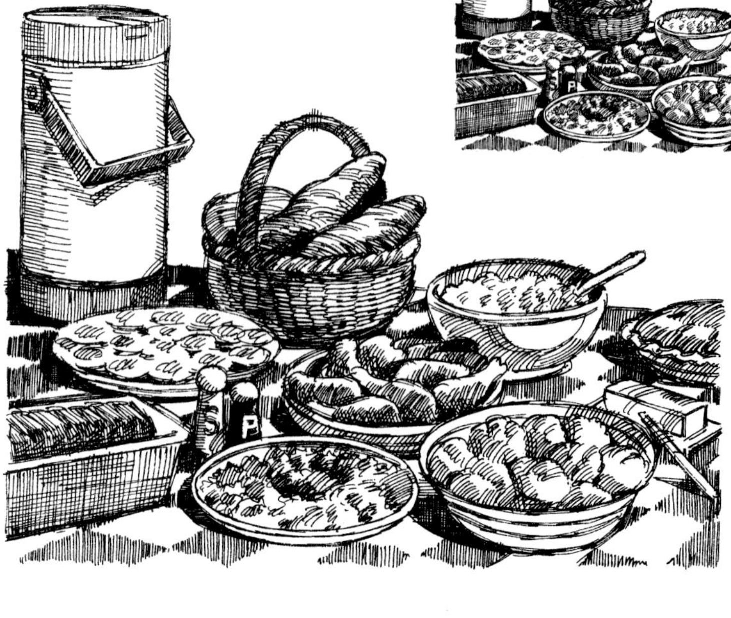

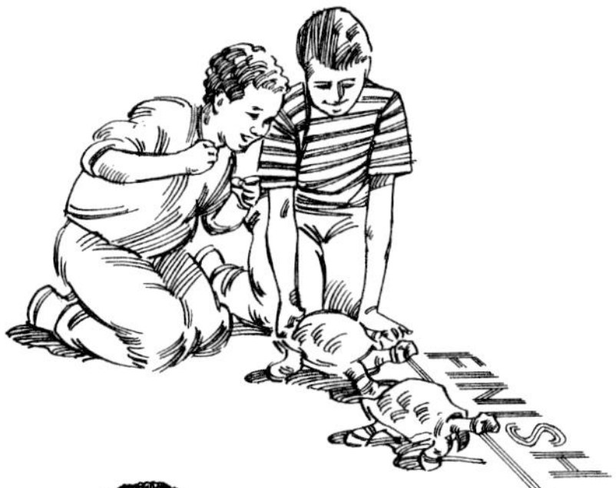
FINISH

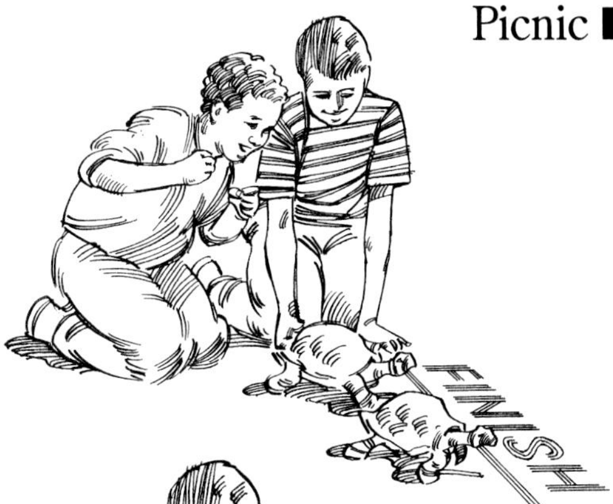
FINISH

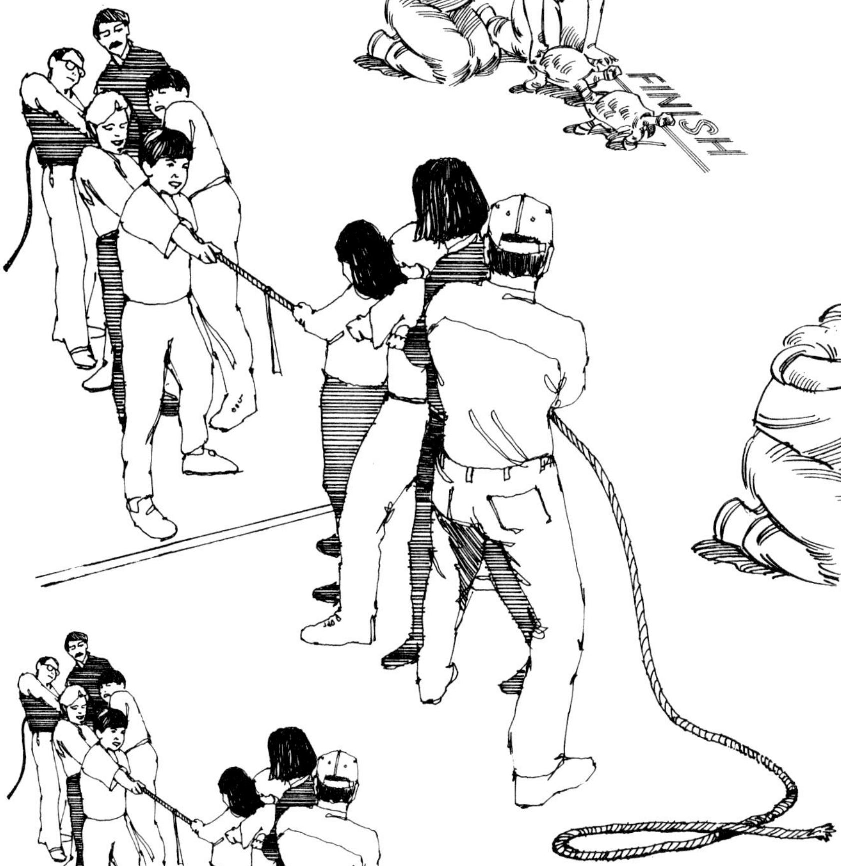

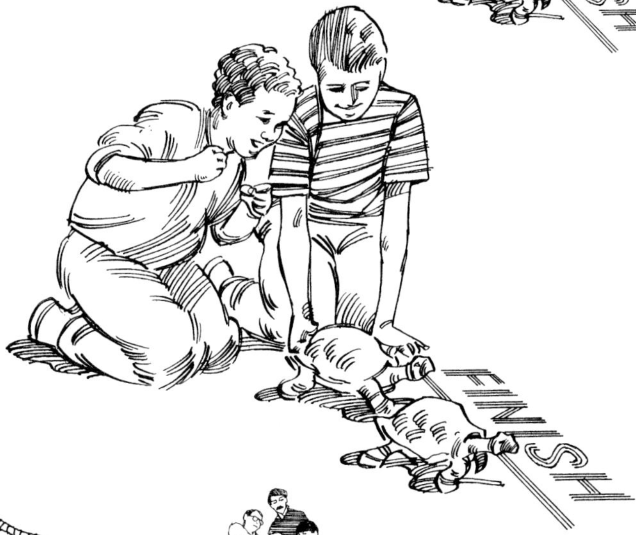
FINISH

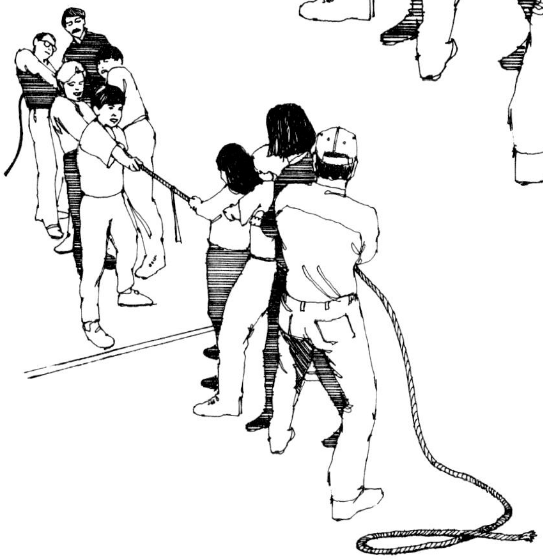

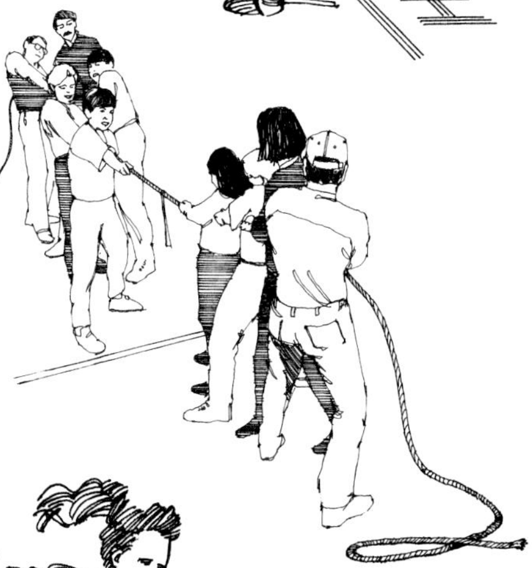

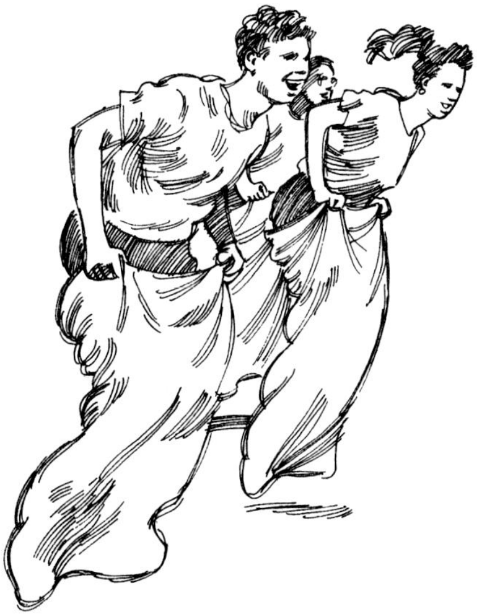

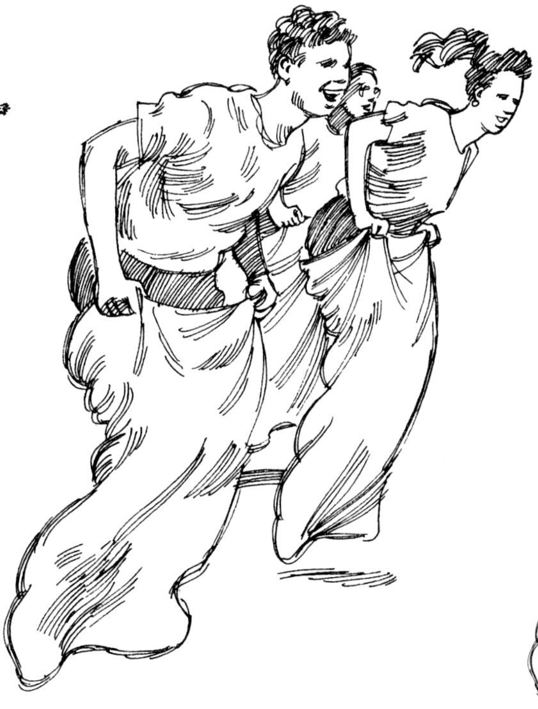

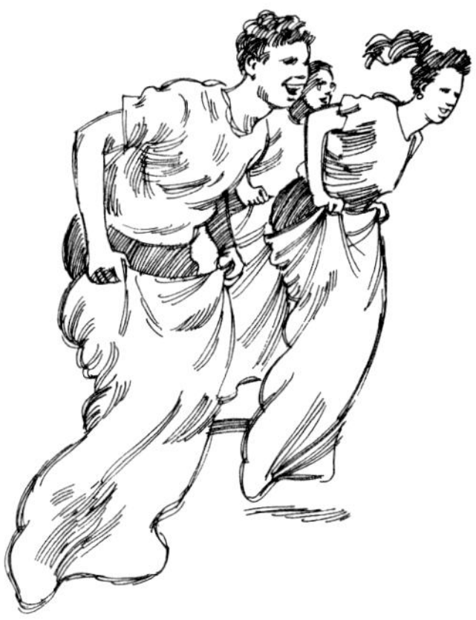

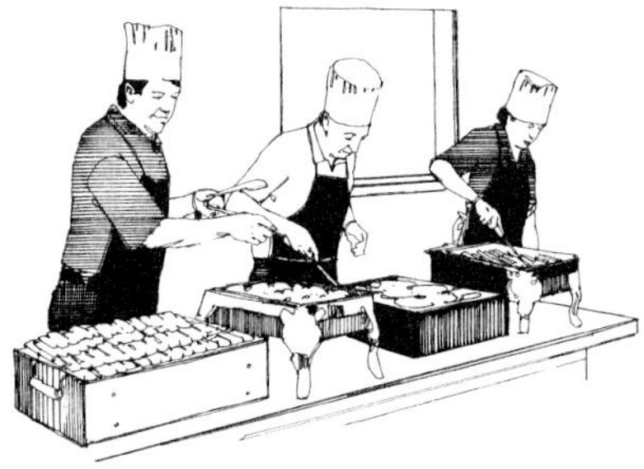

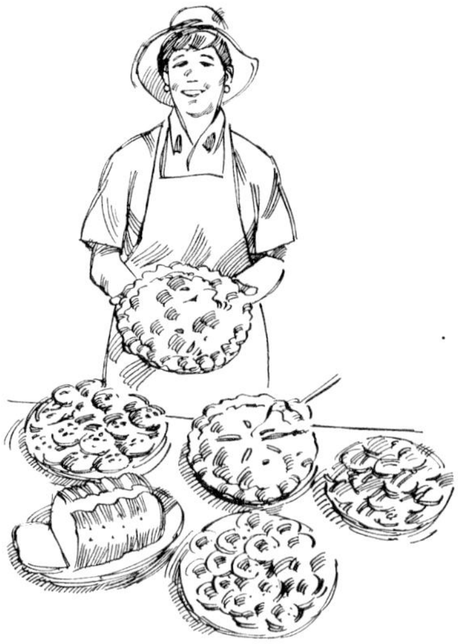

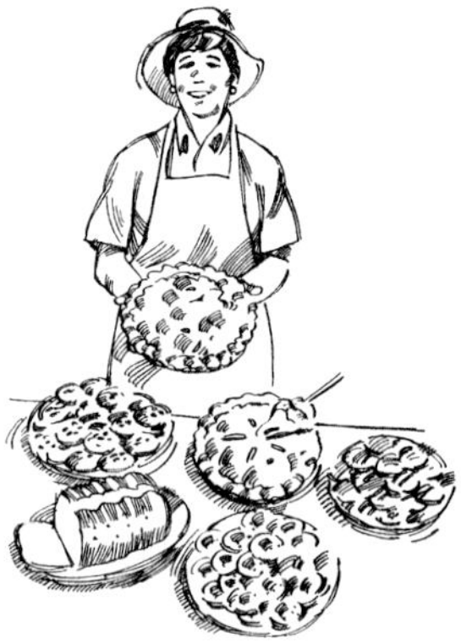

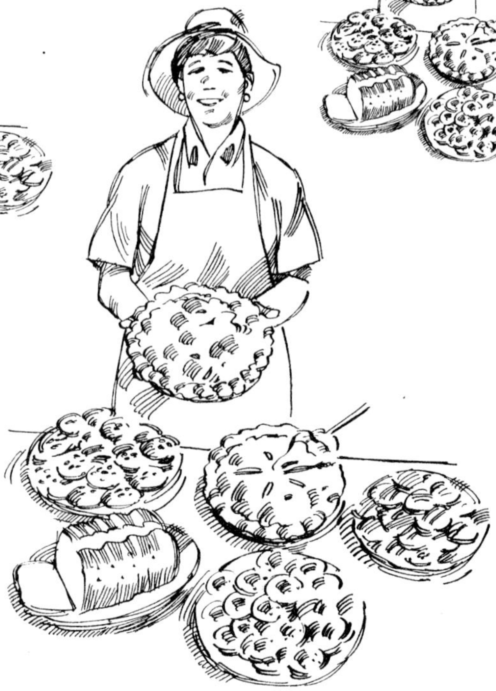

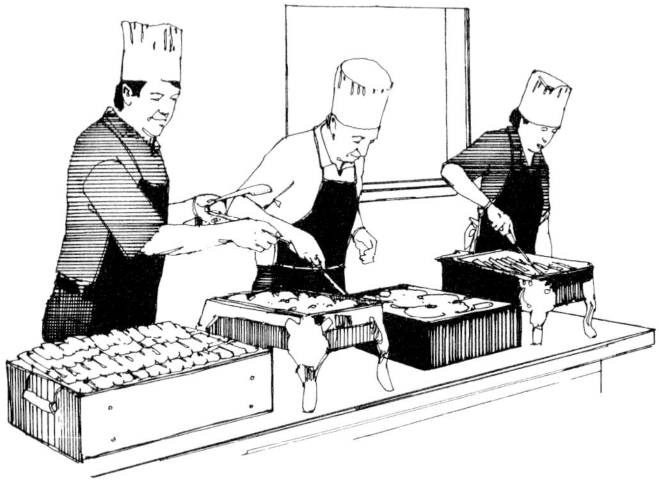

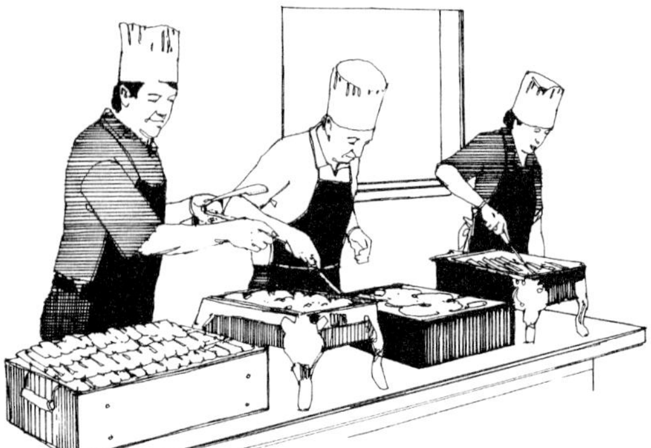

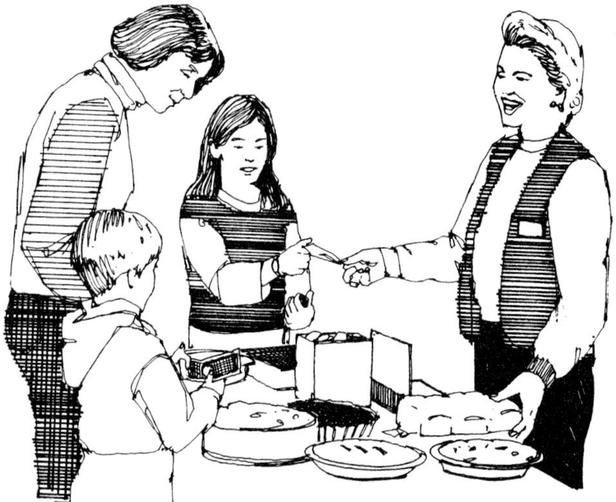

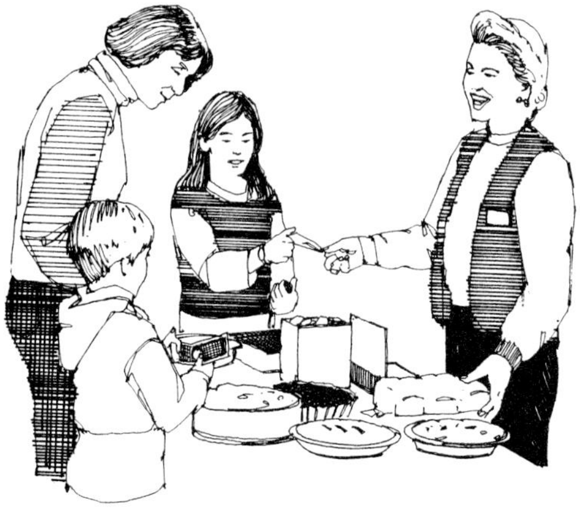

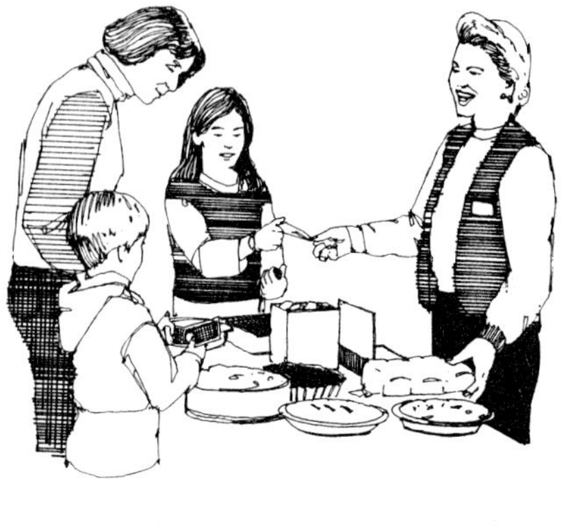

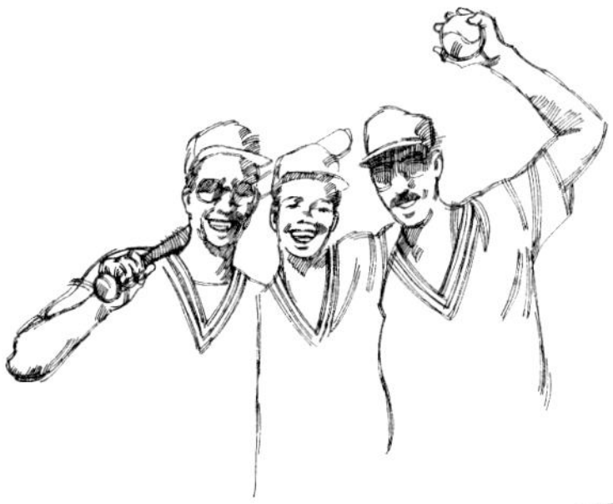

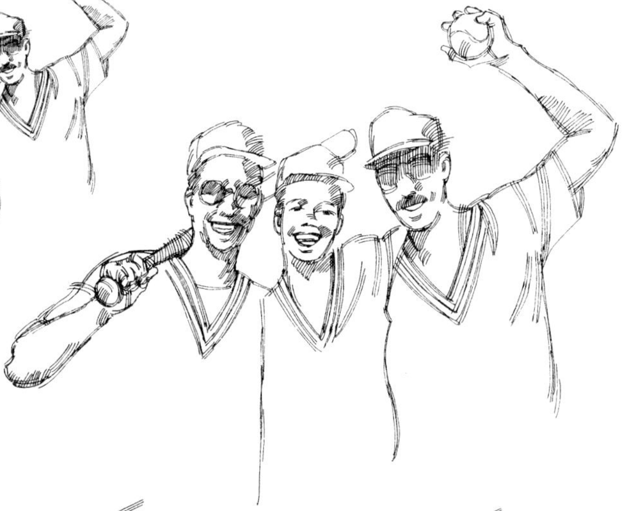

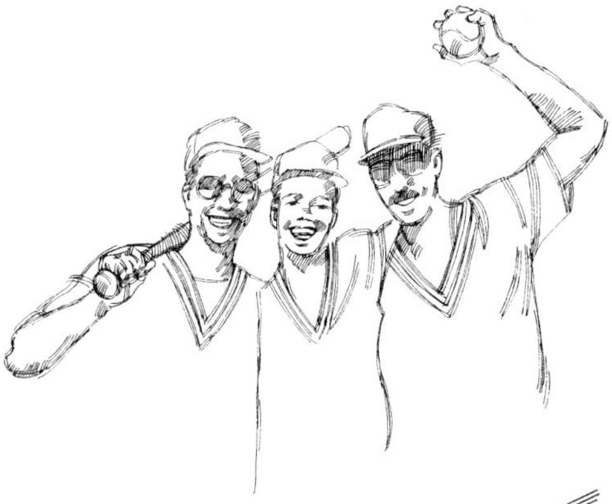

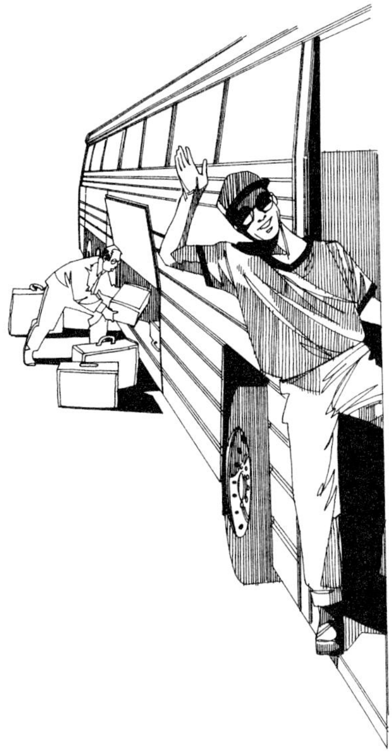

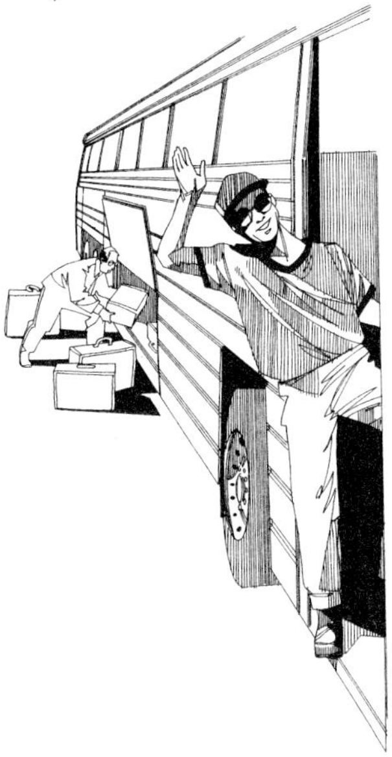

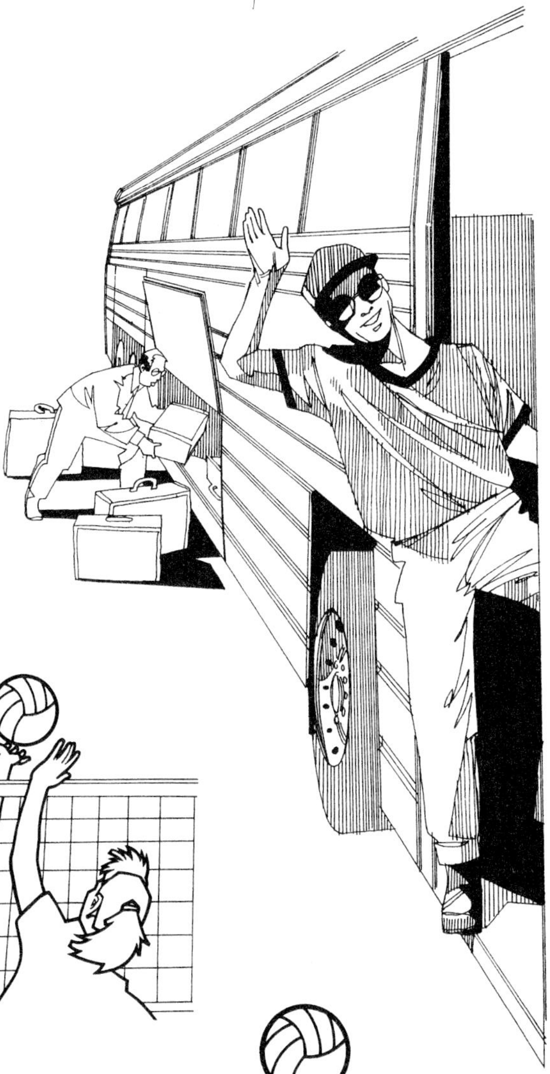

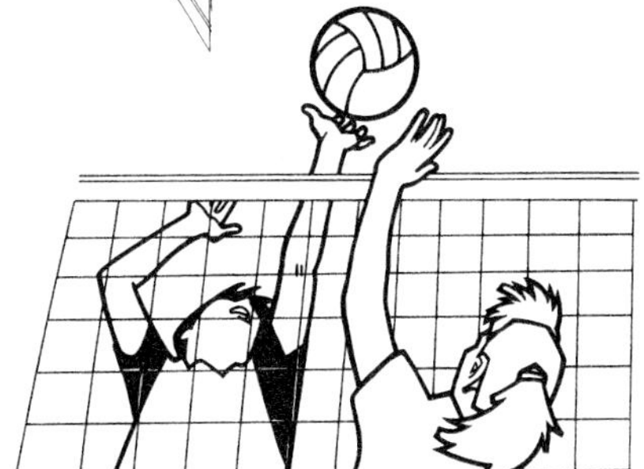

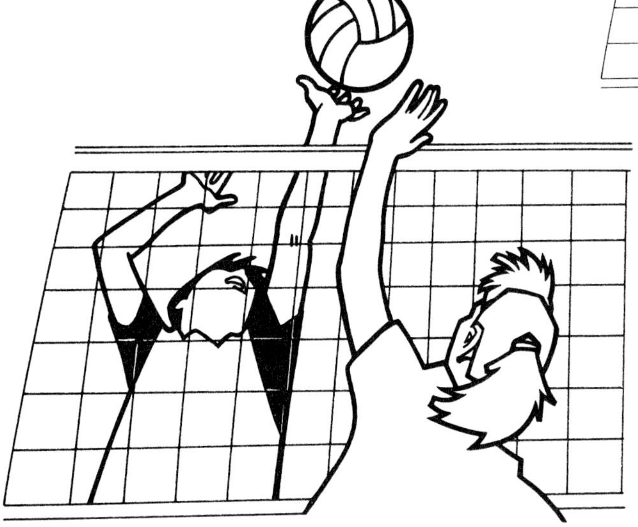

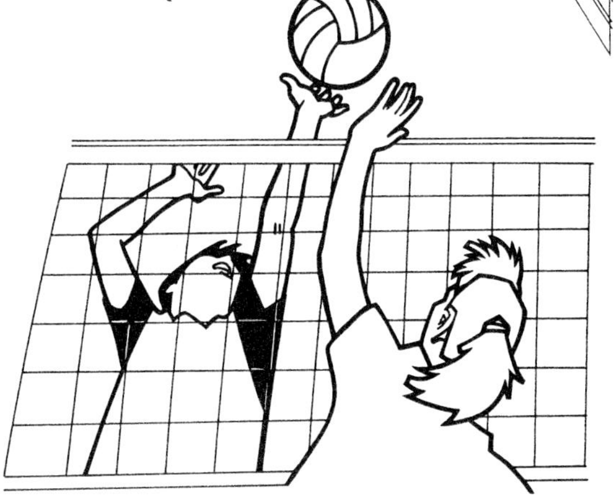

■ Church and School

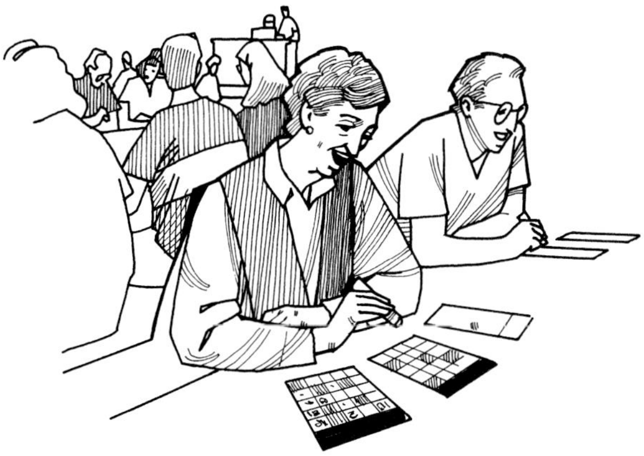

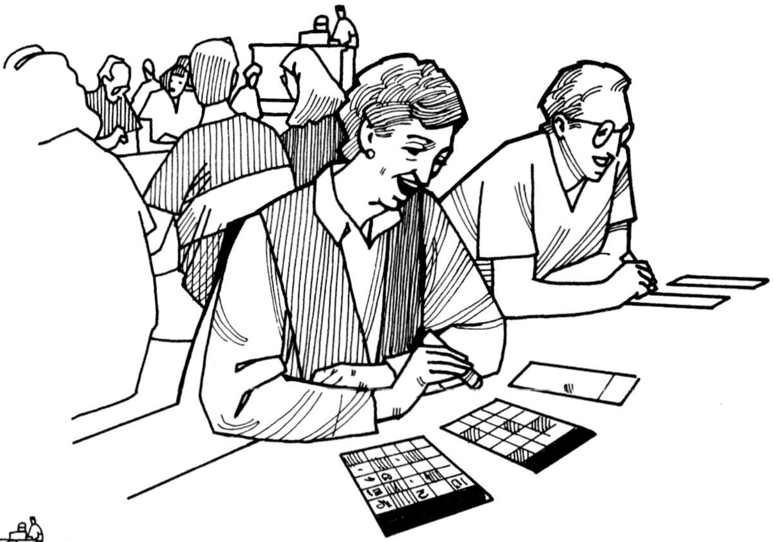

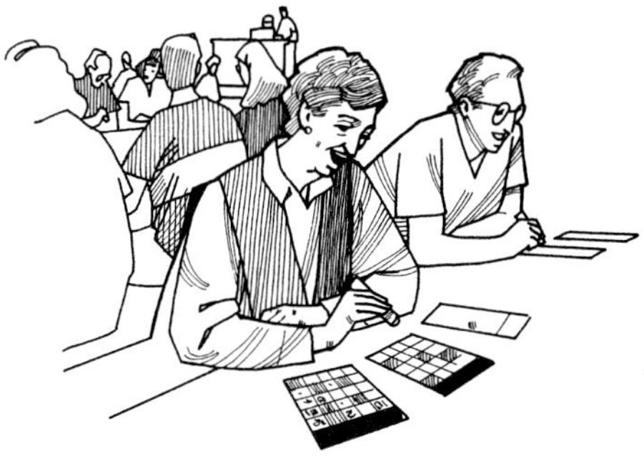

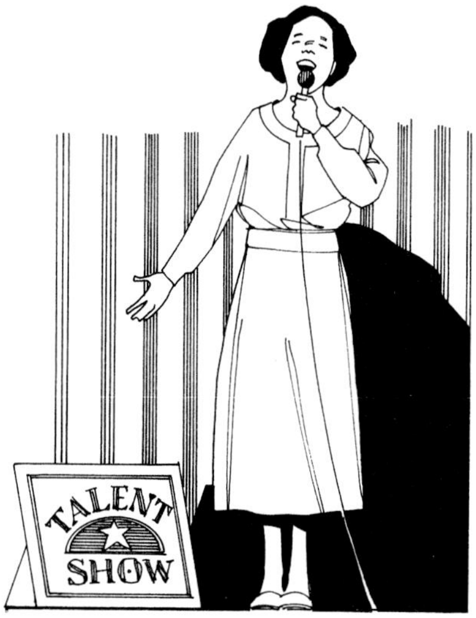

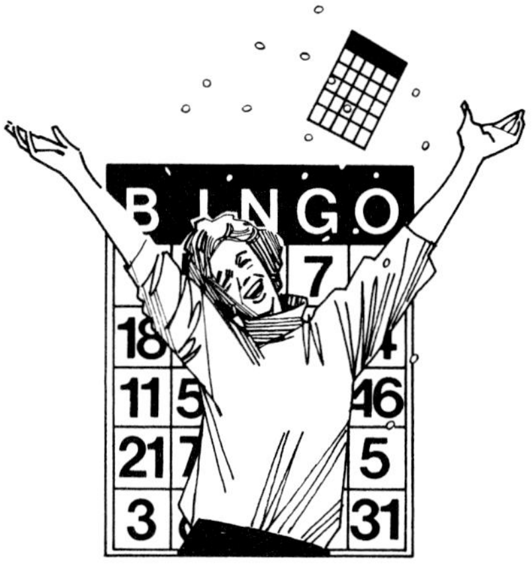

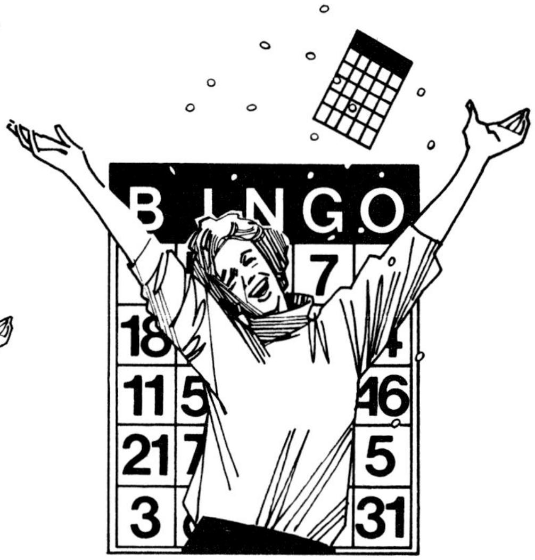

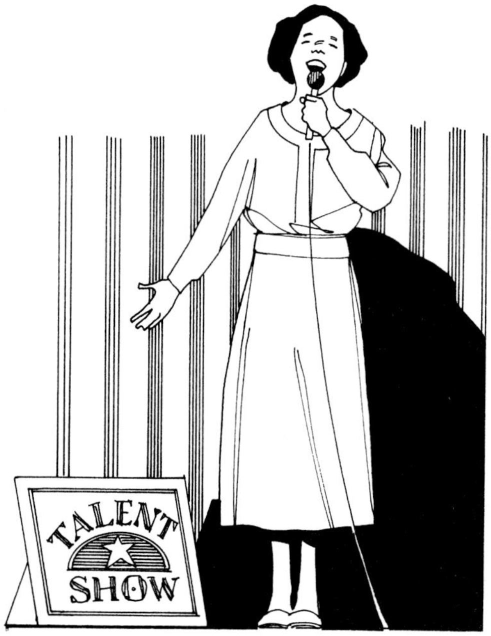

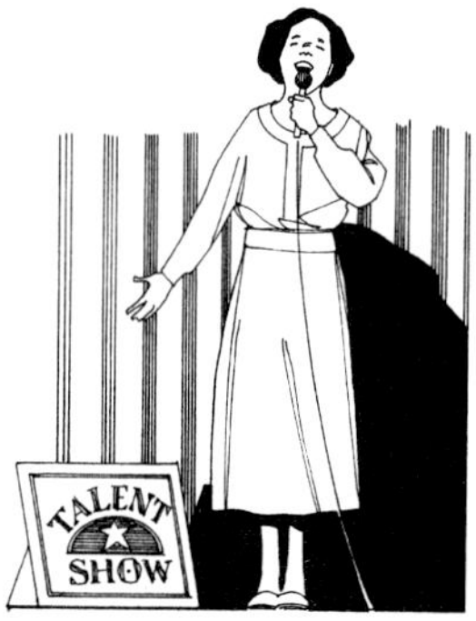

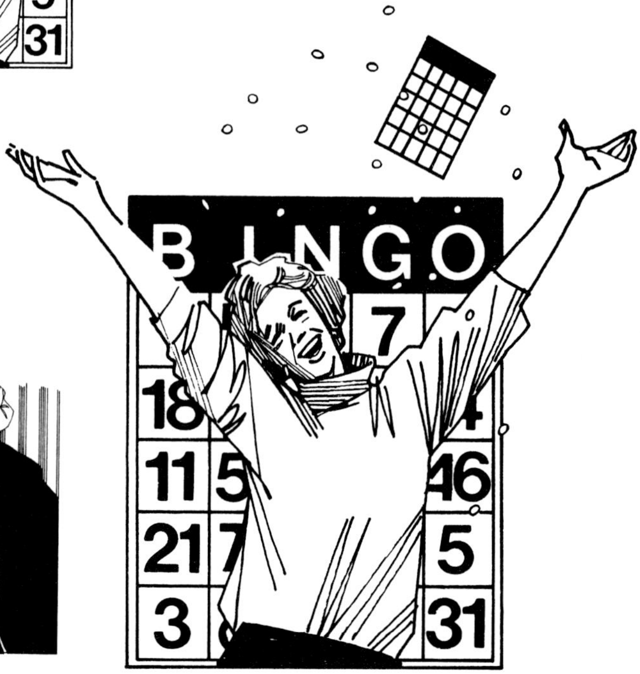

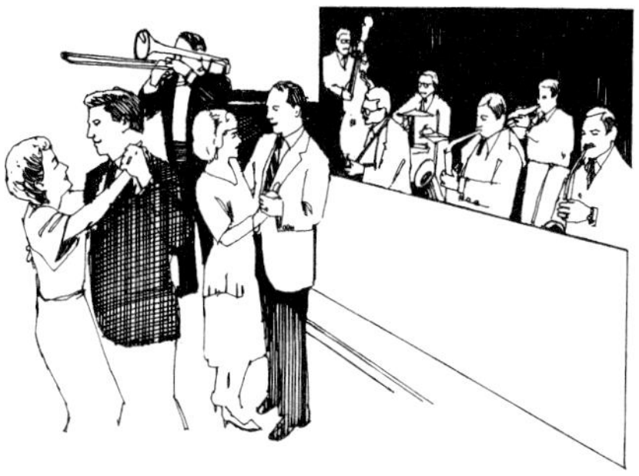

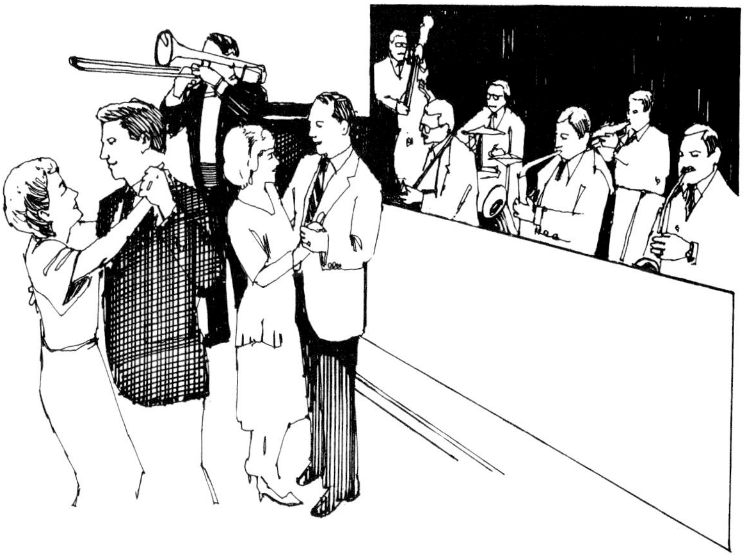

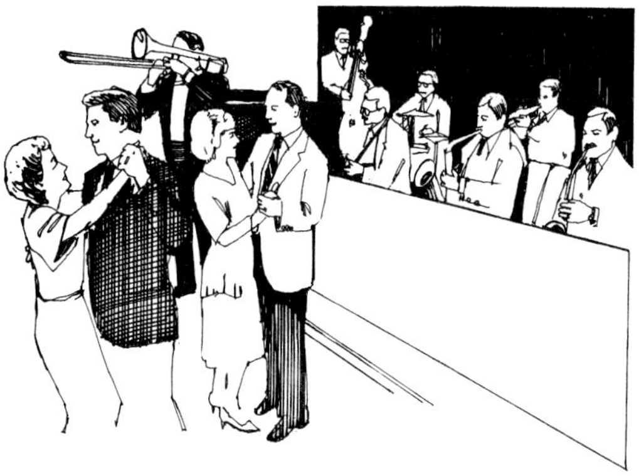

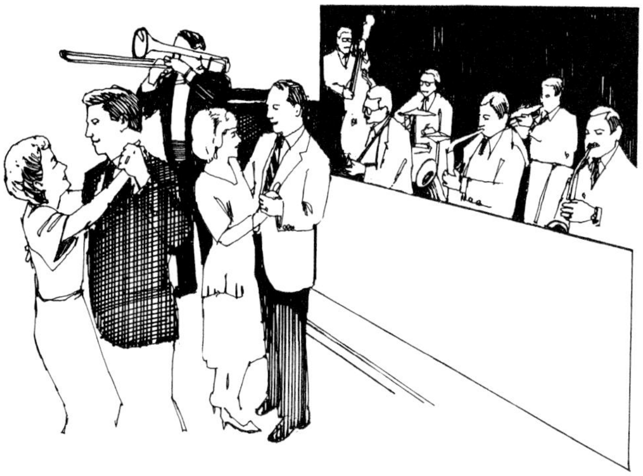

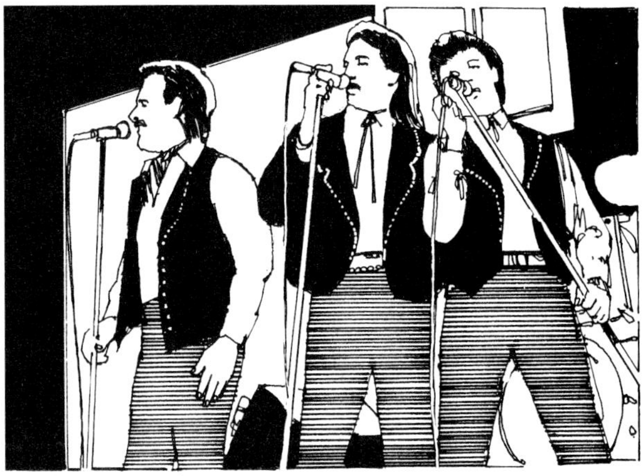

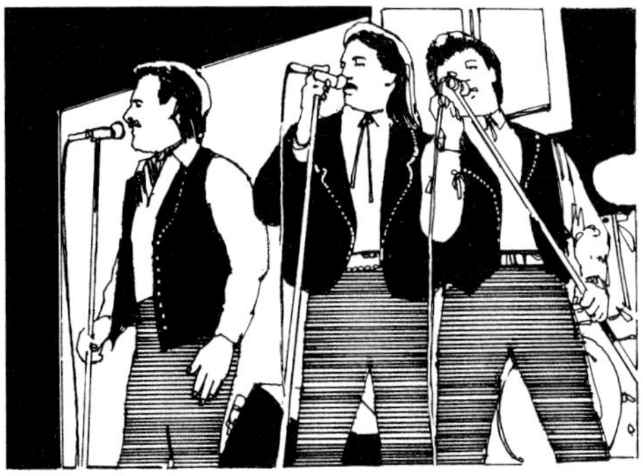

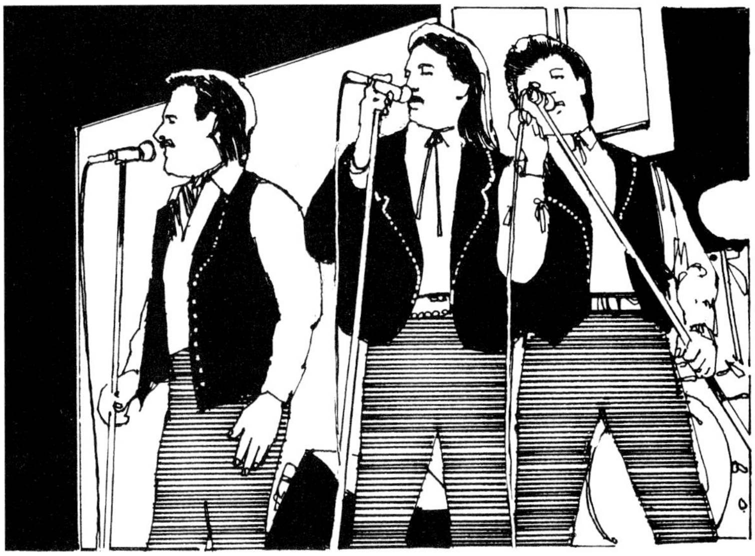

■ Business and Civic

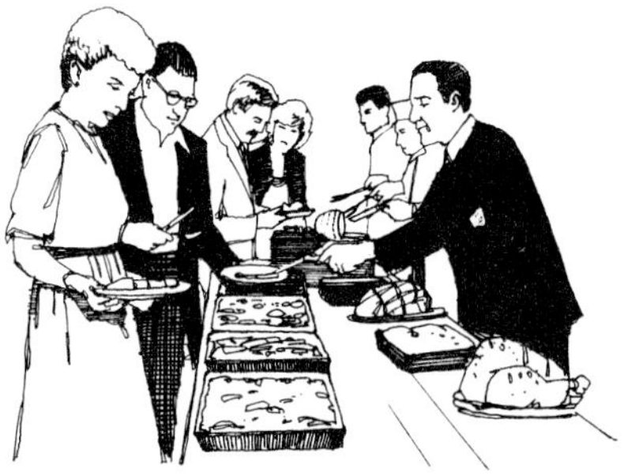

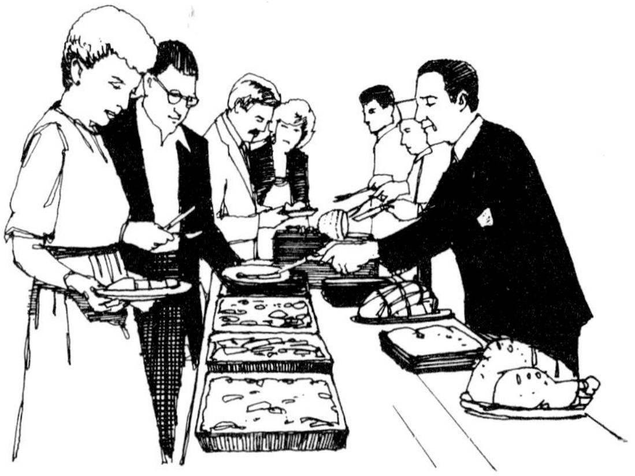

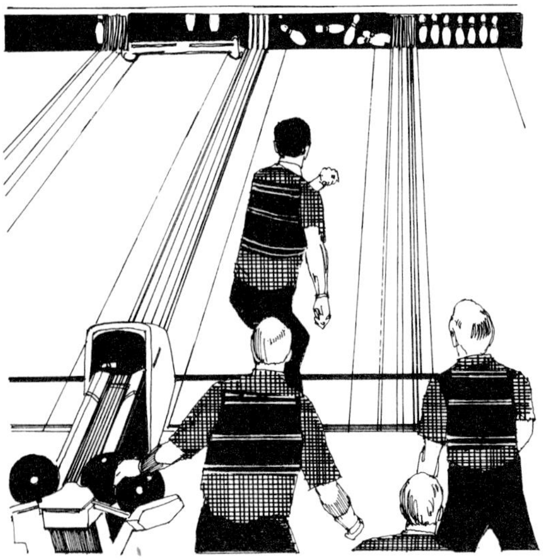

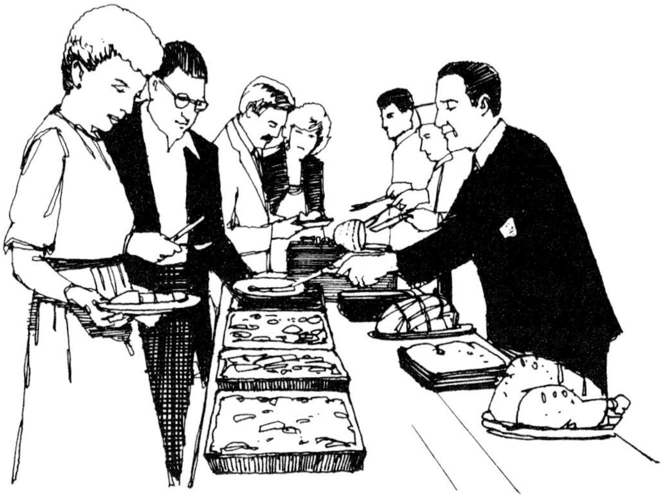

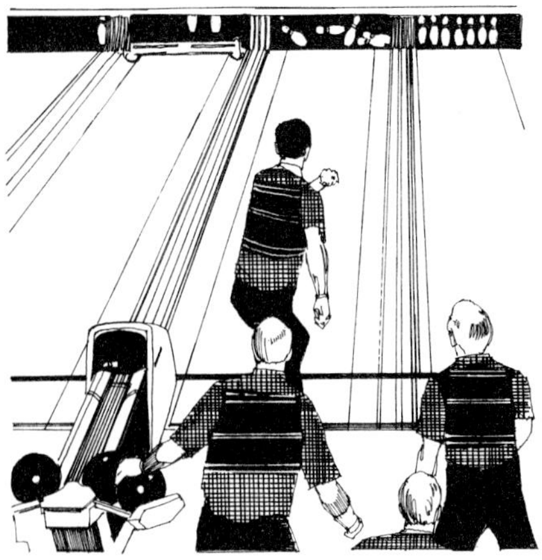

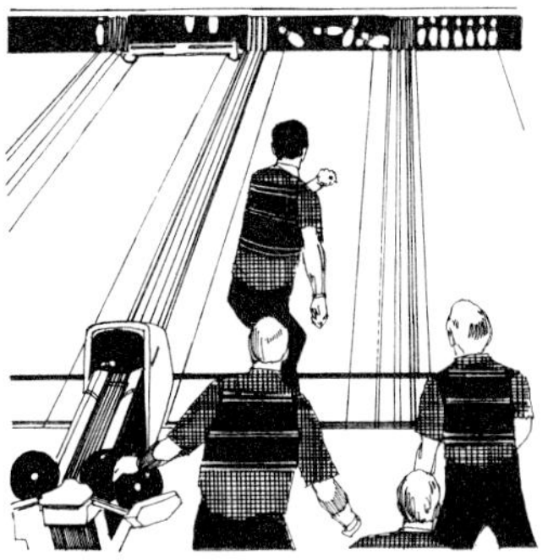

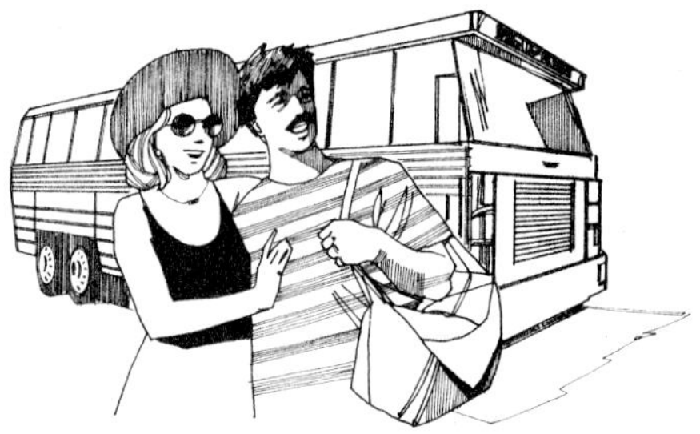

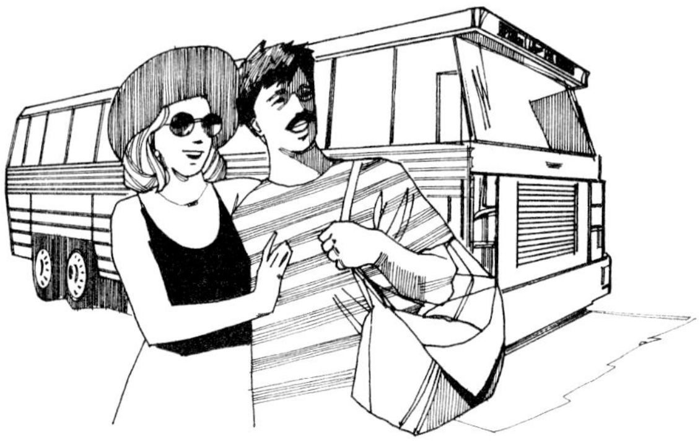

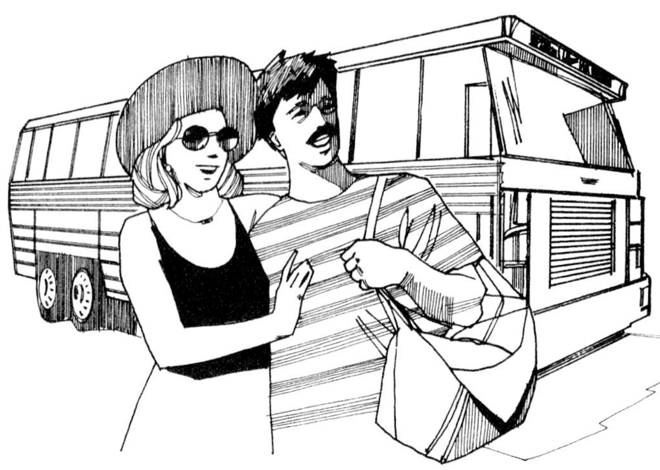

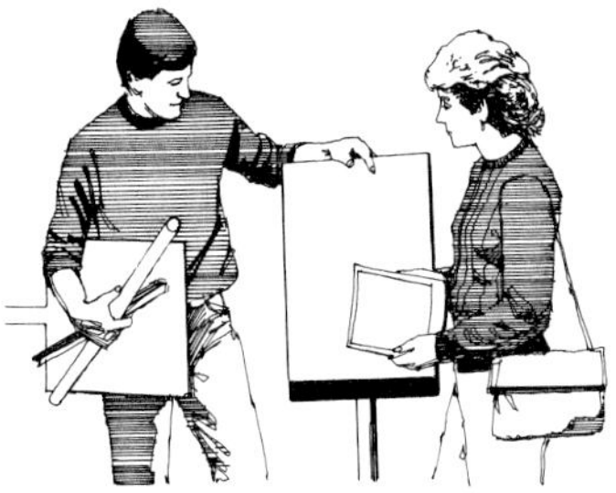

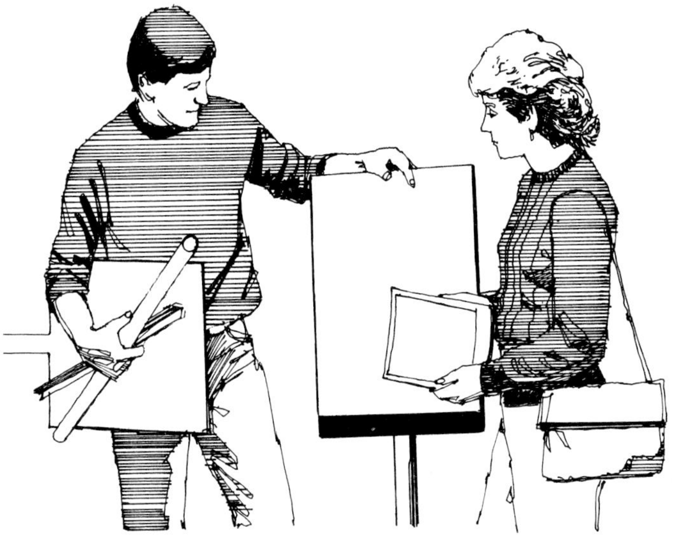

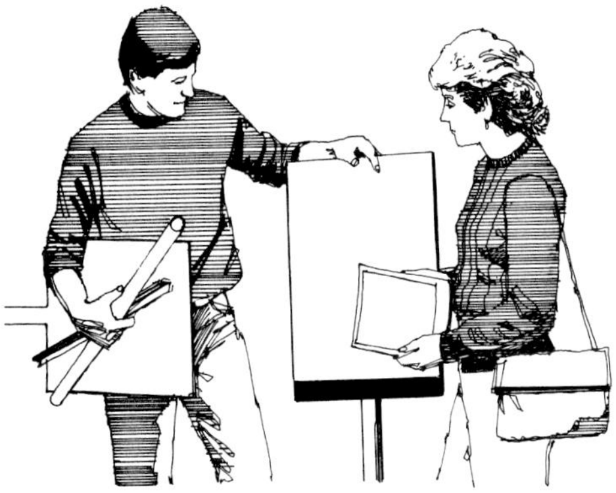

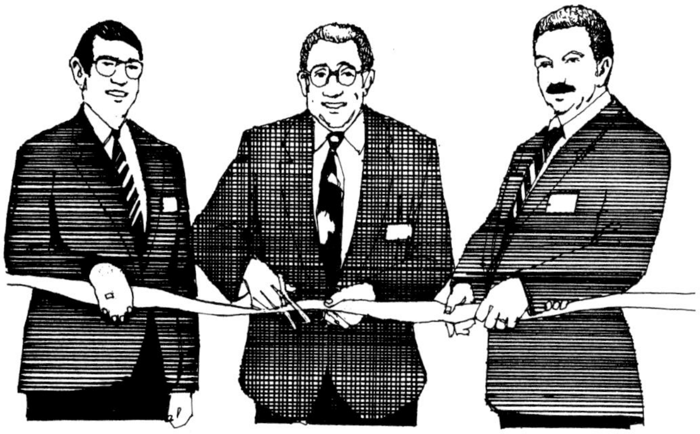

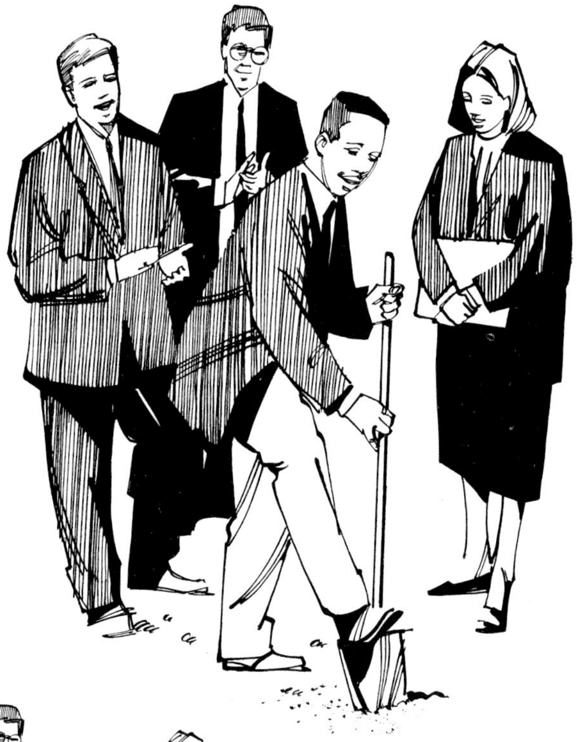

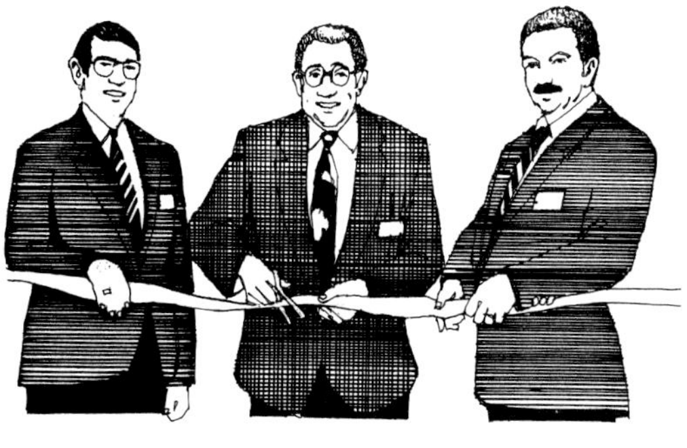

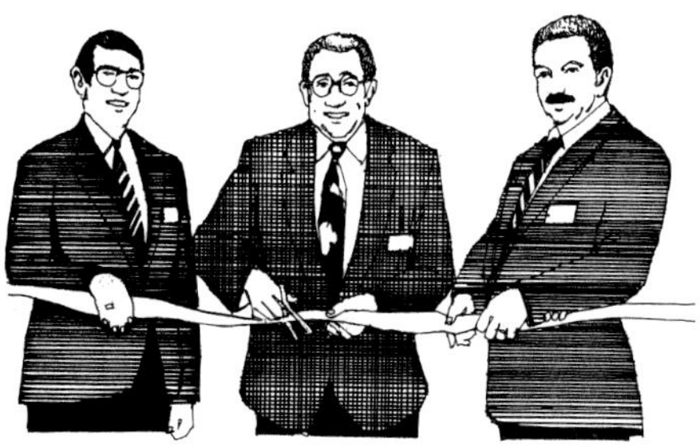

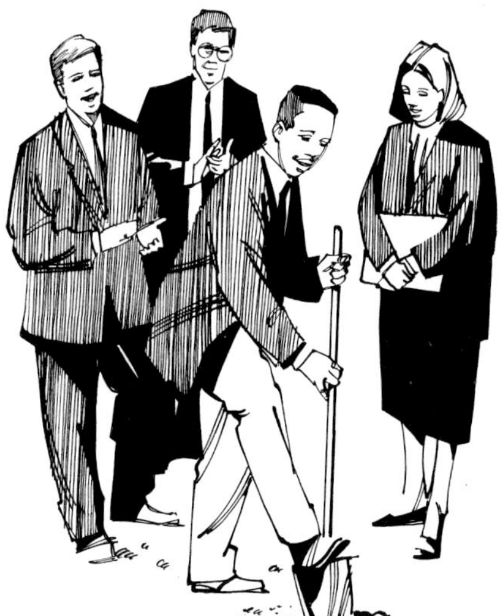

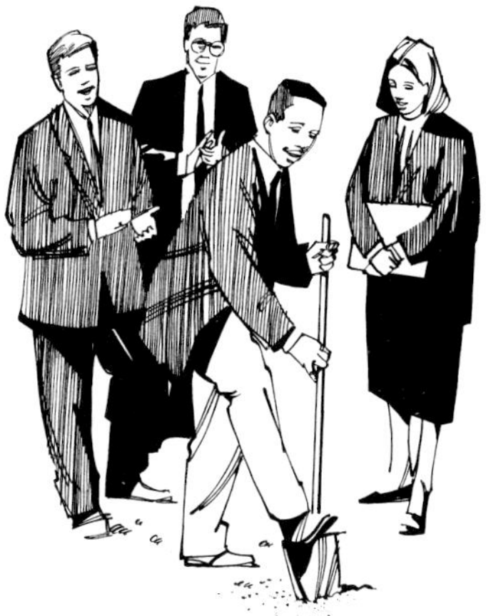

Business and Civic

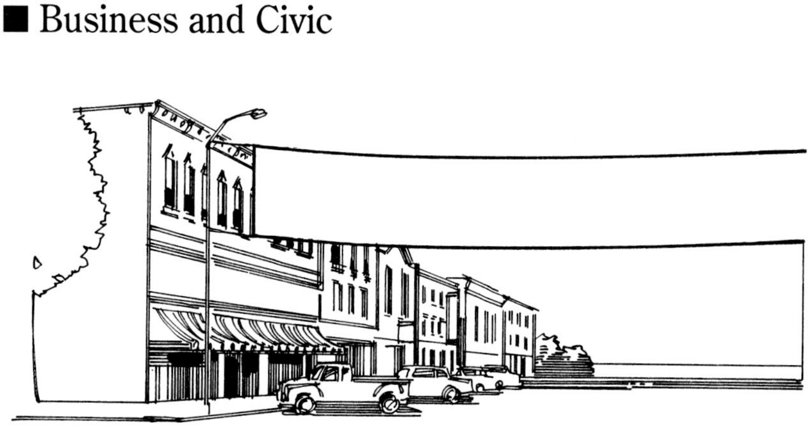

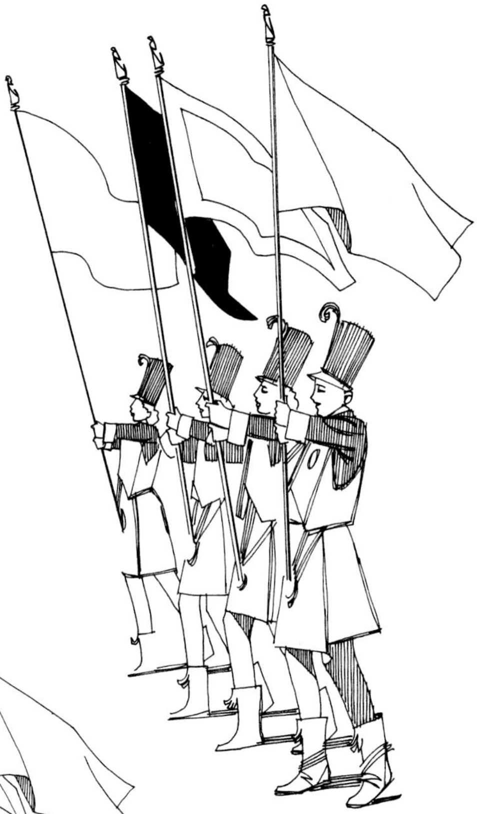

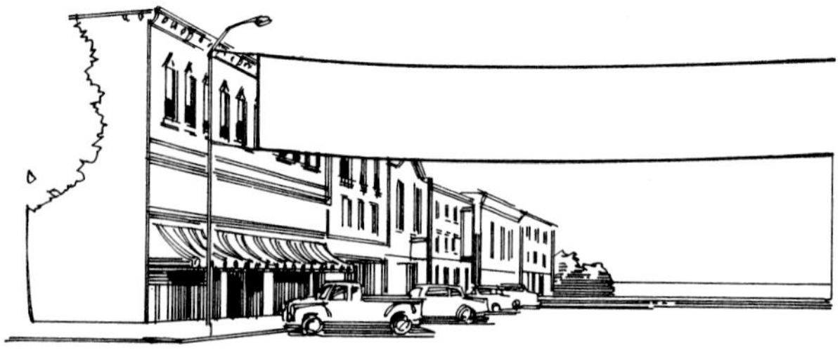

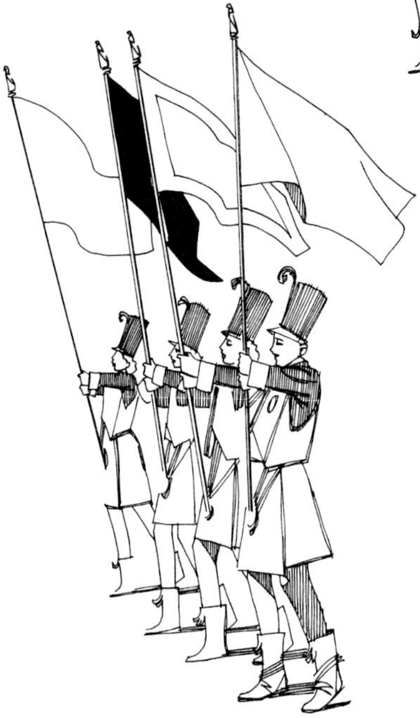

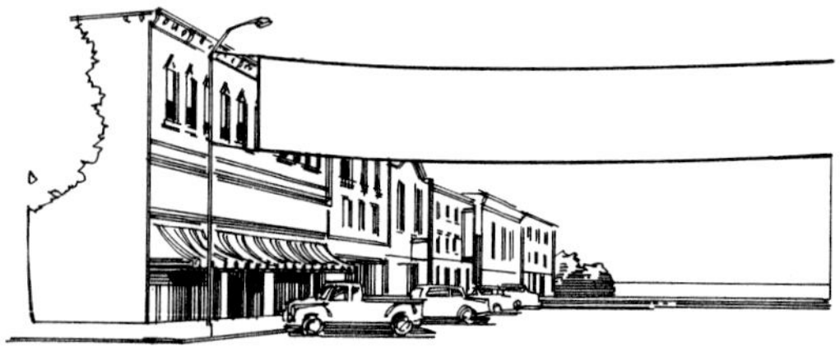

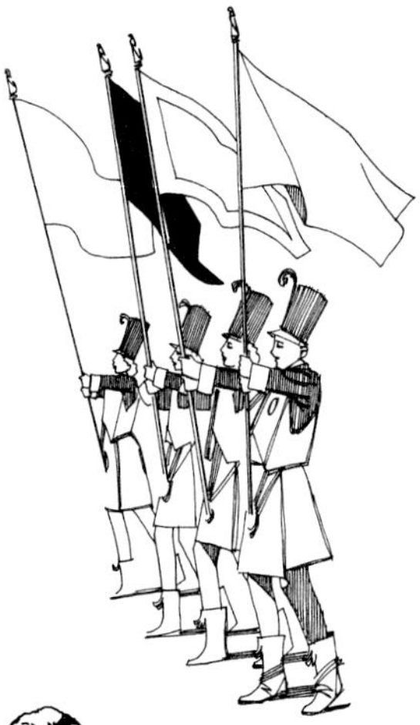

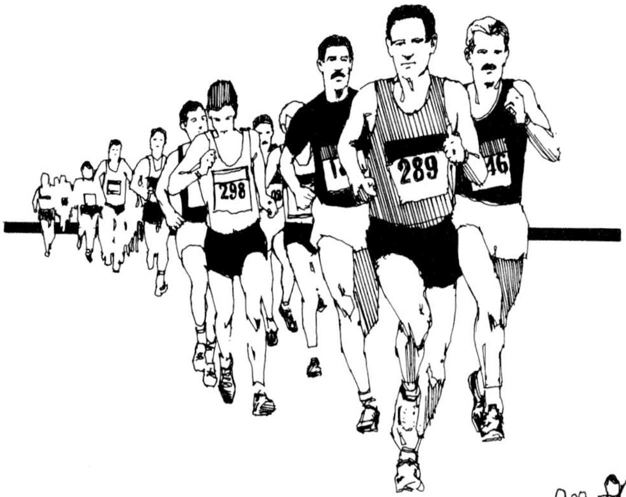

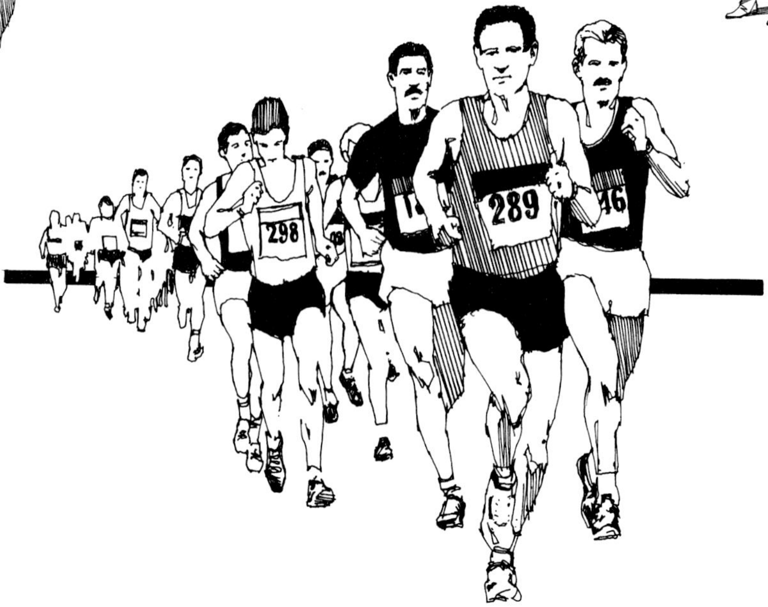

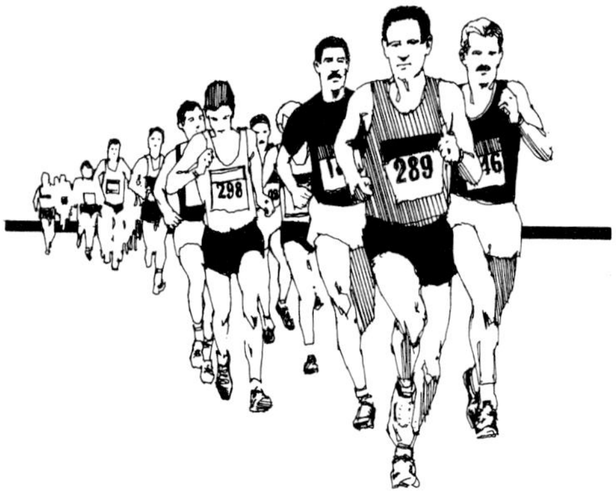

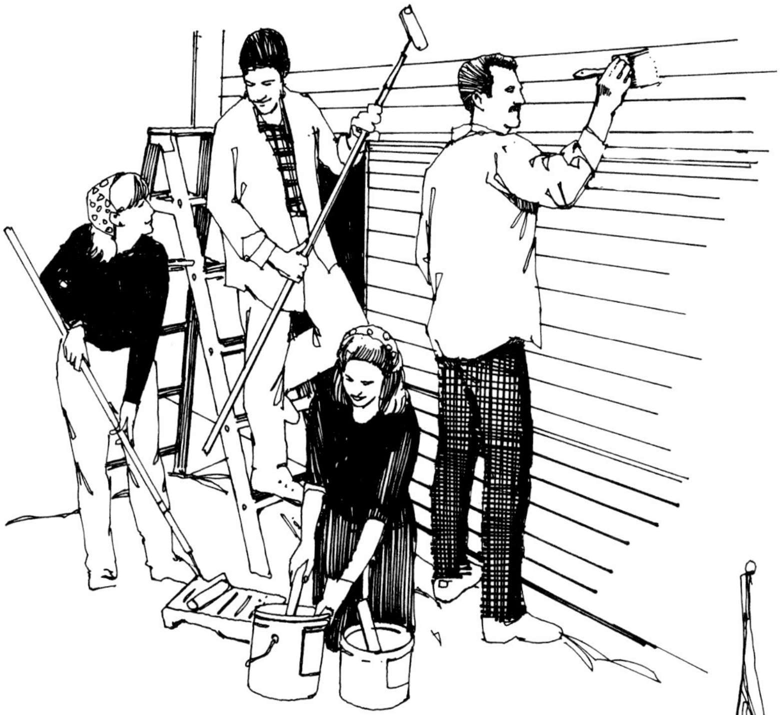

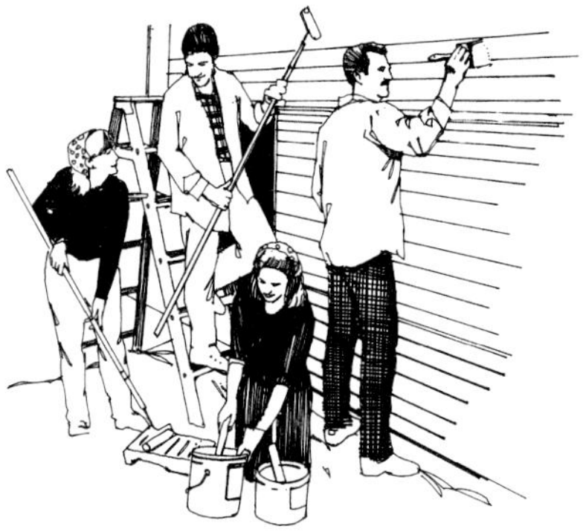

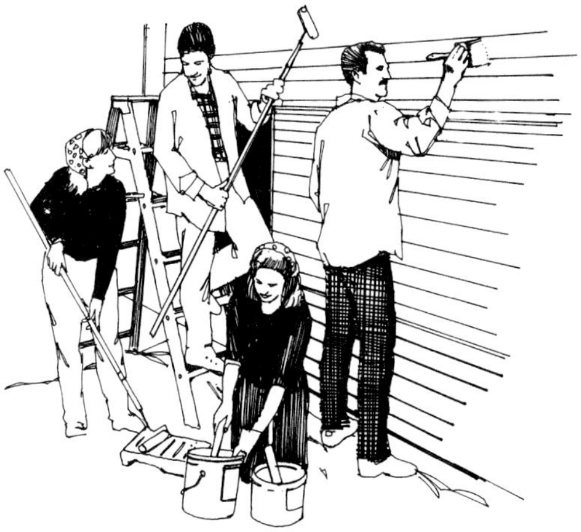

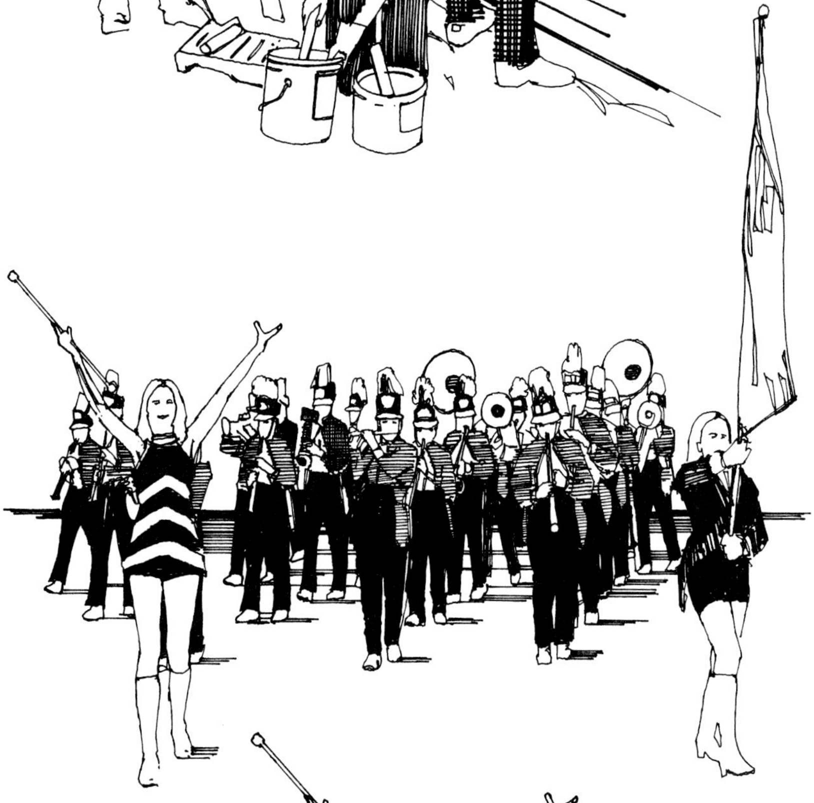

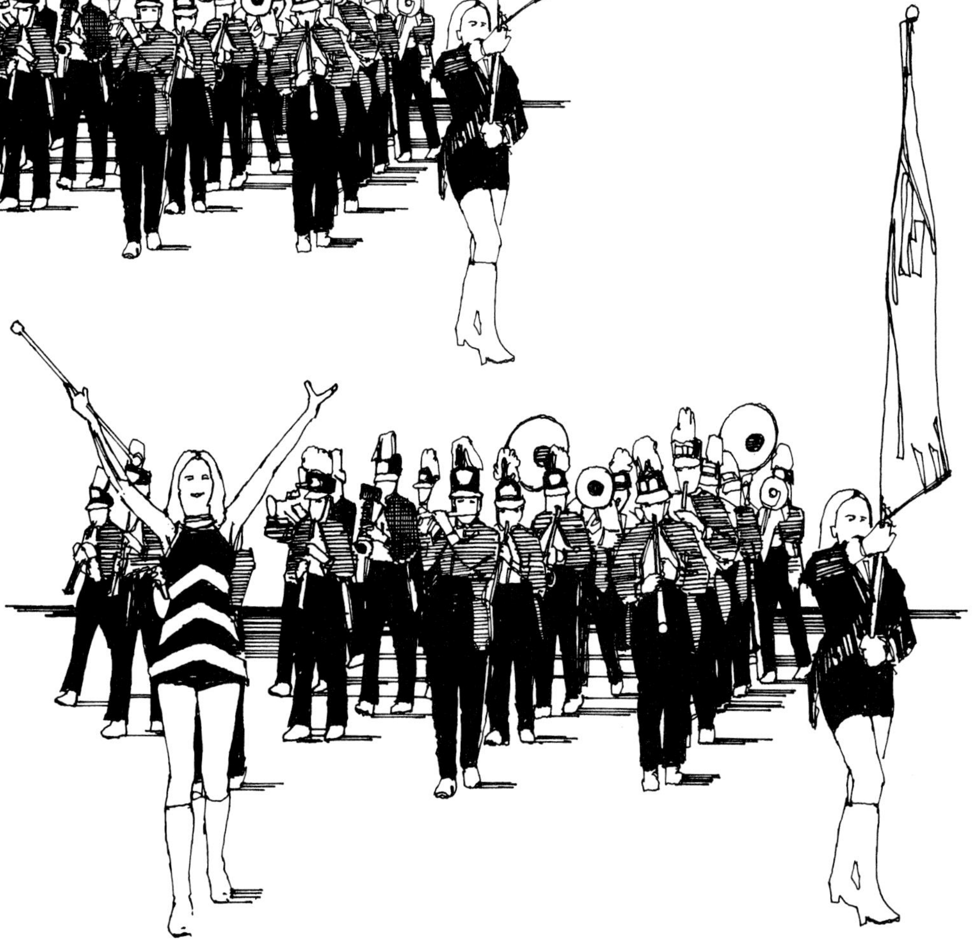

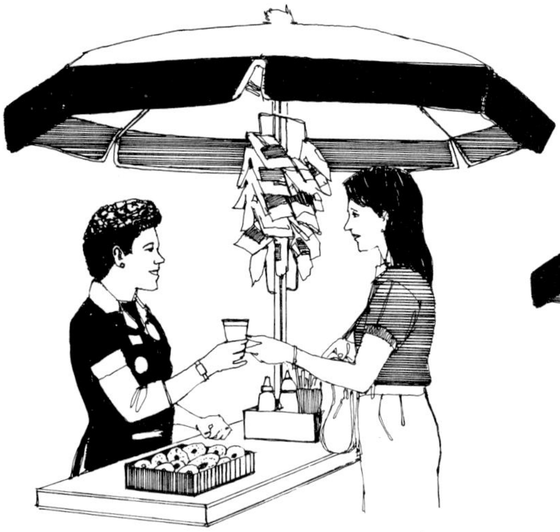

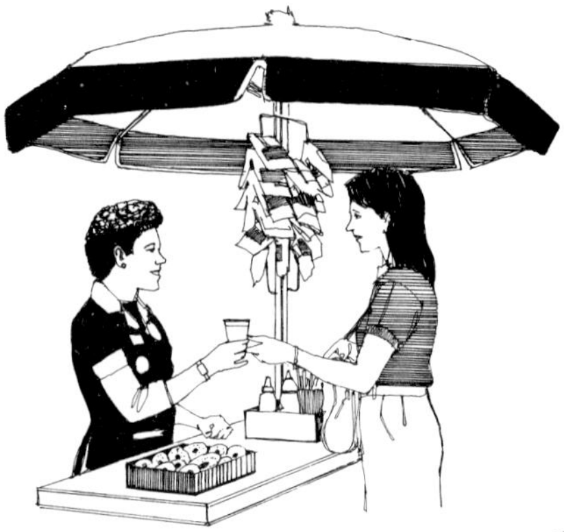

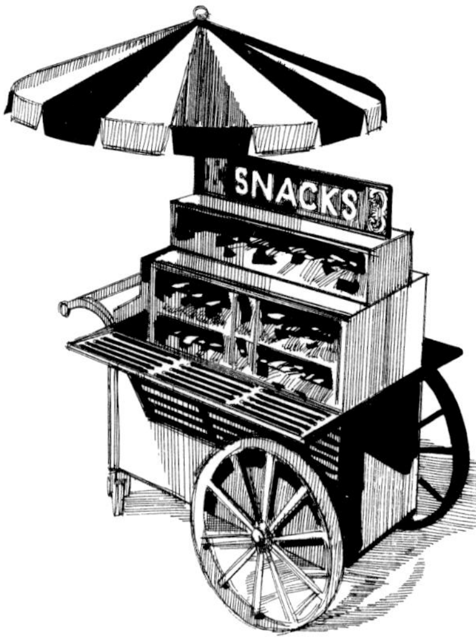
SNACKS

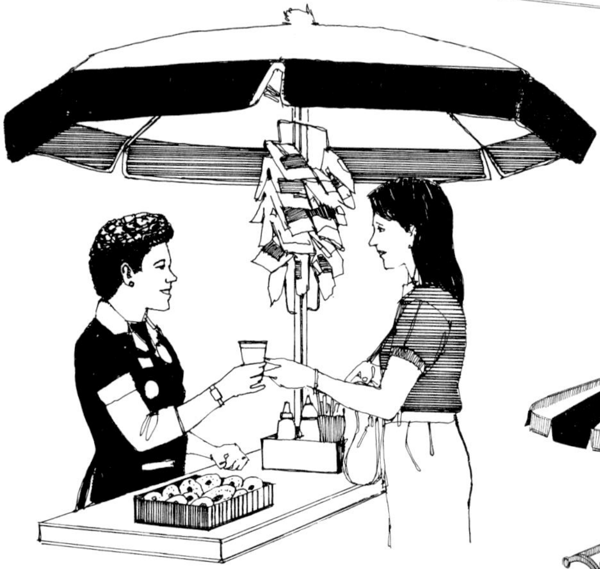

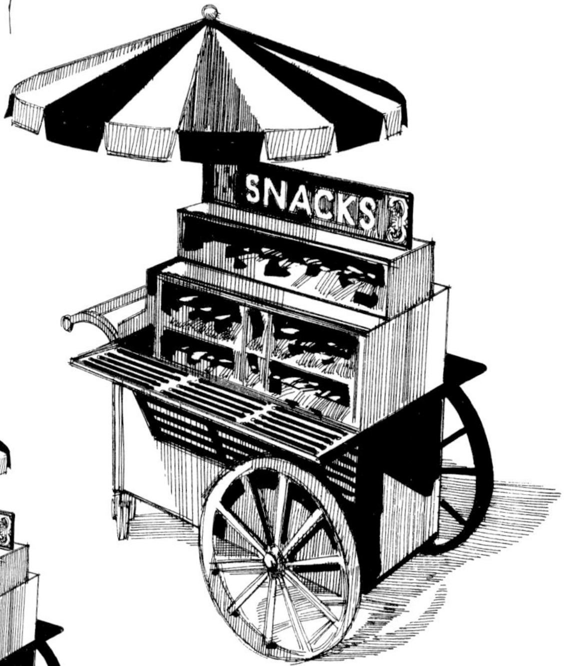
SNACKS

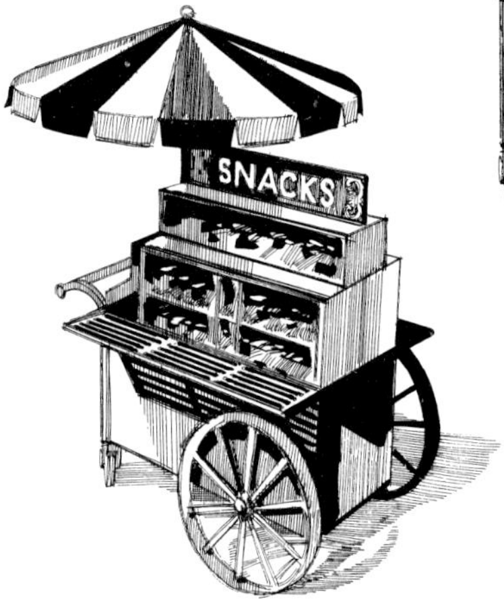
SNACKS

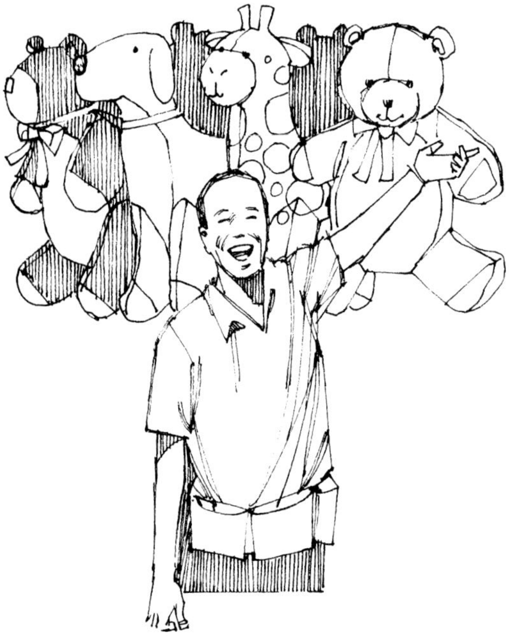

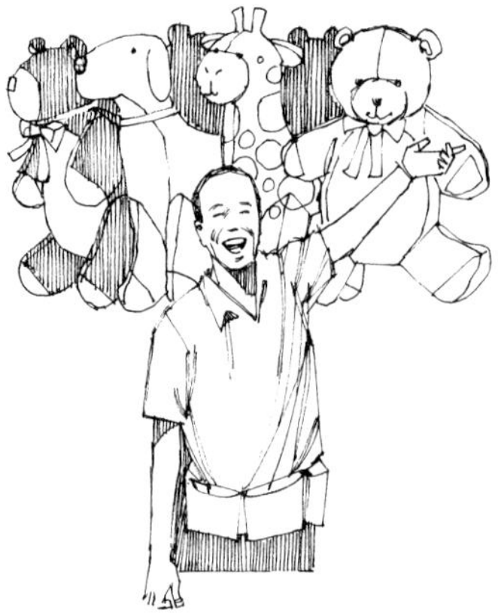

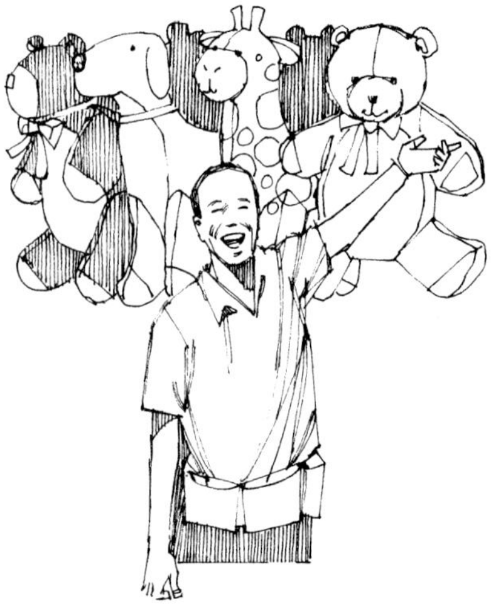

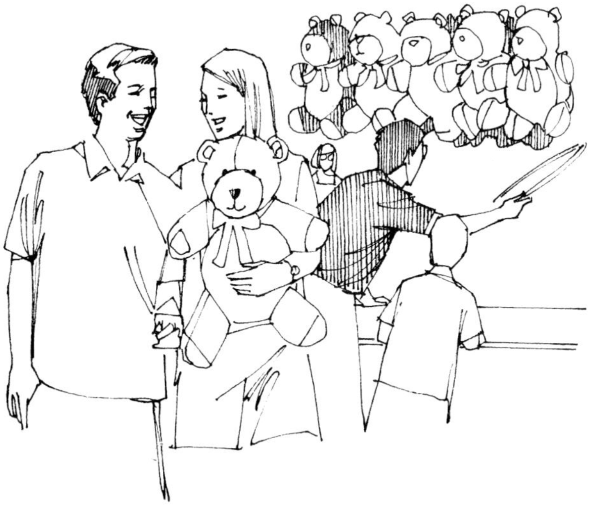

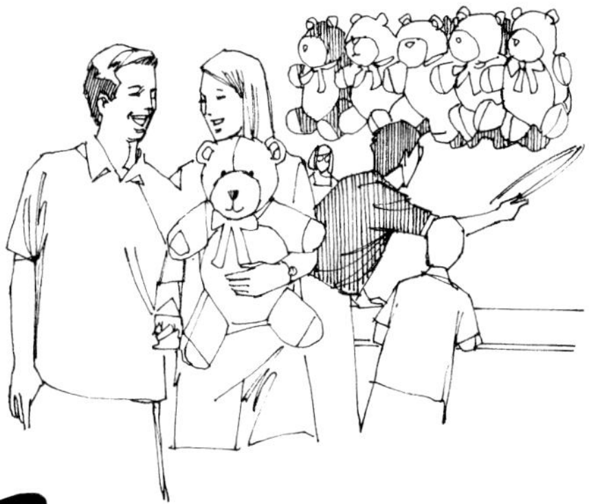

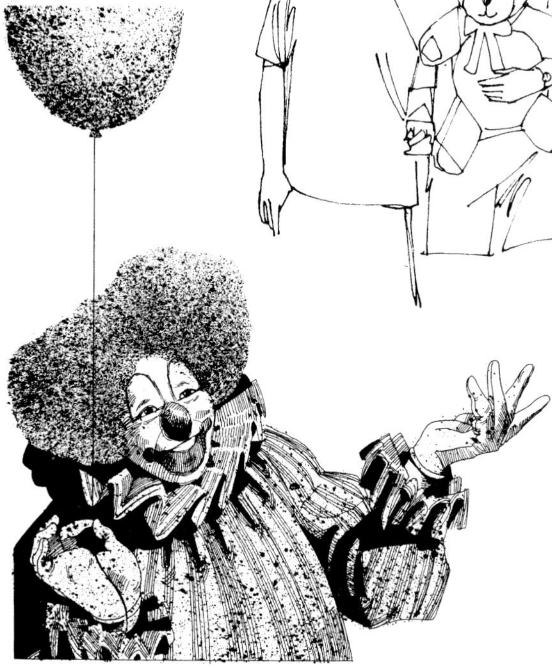

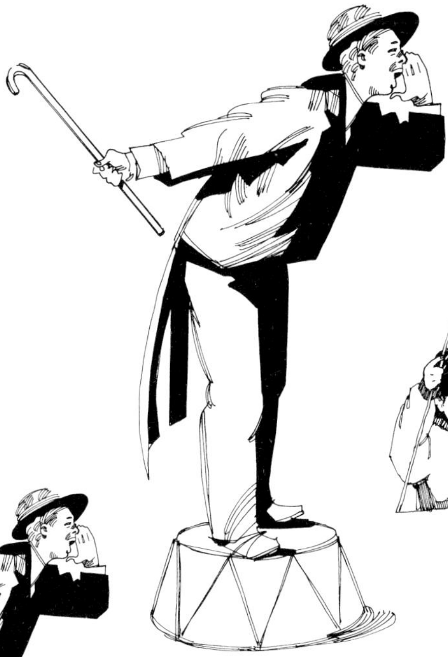

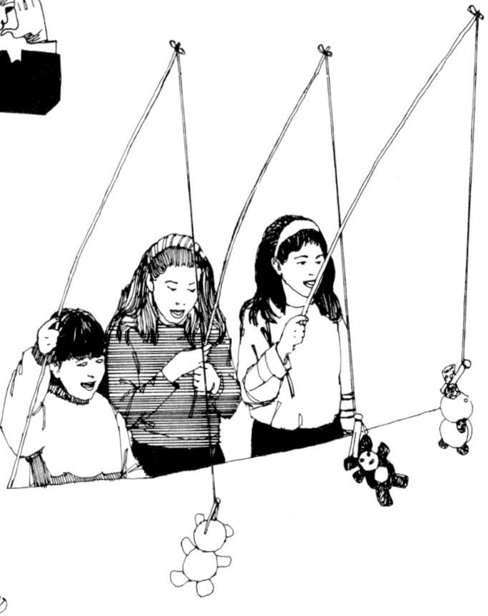

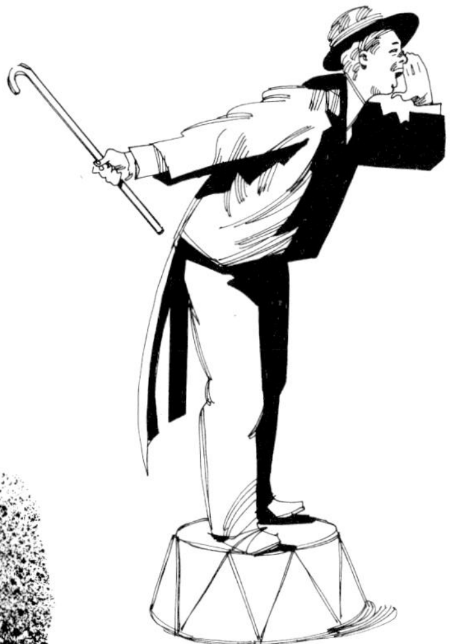

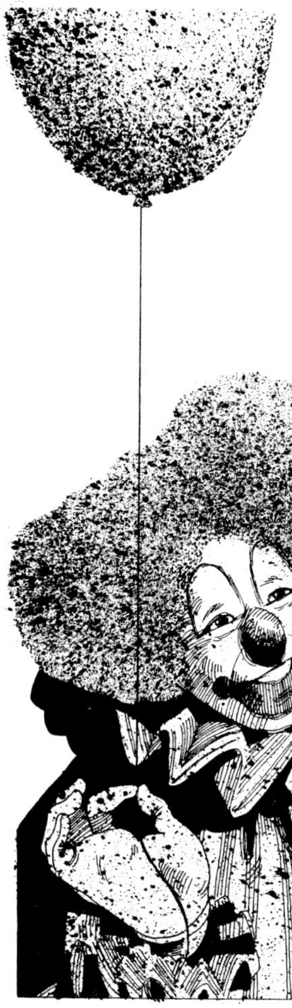

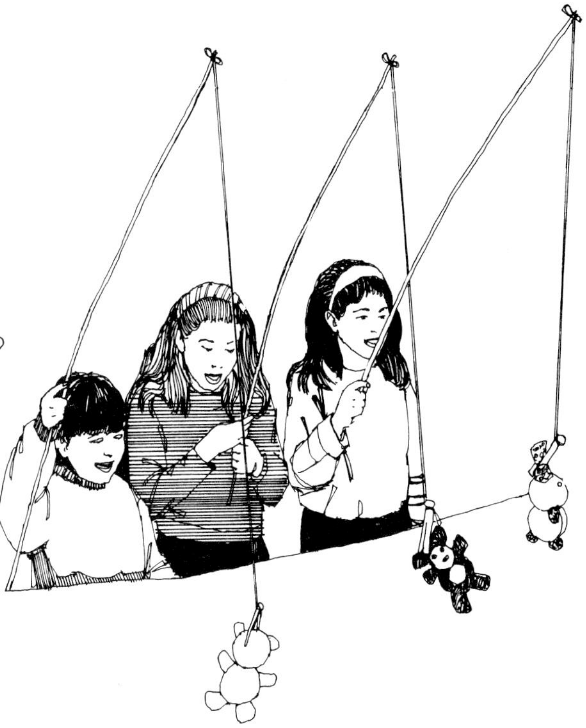

■ Carnivals and Festivals

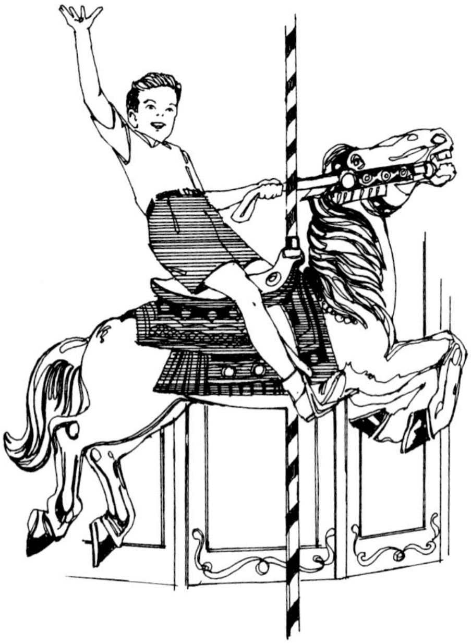

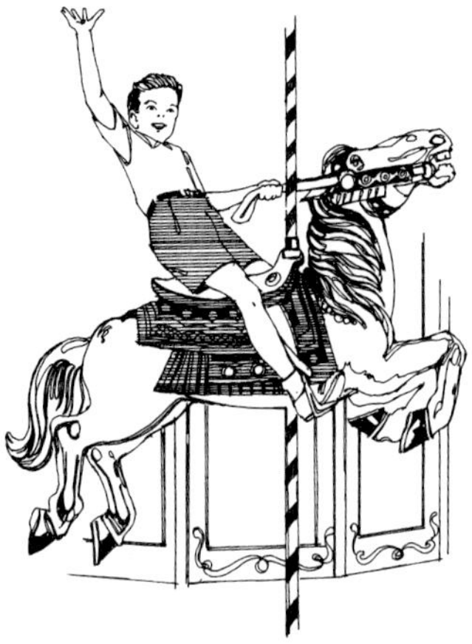

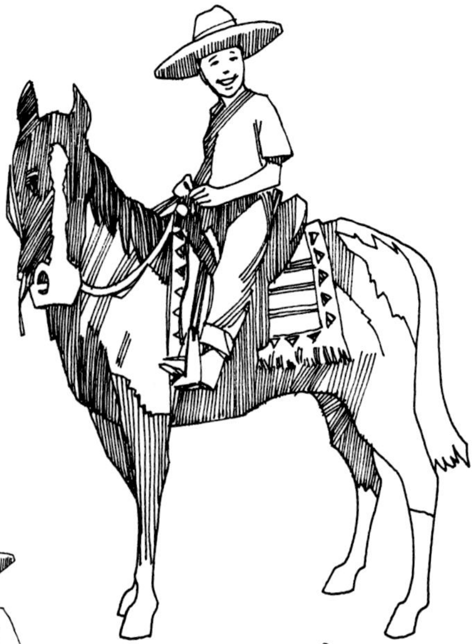

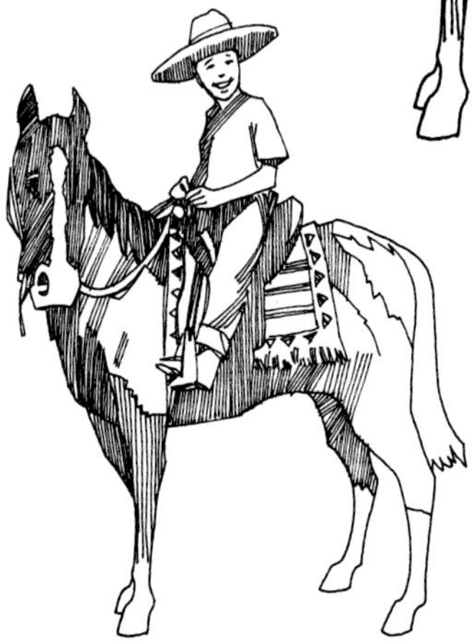

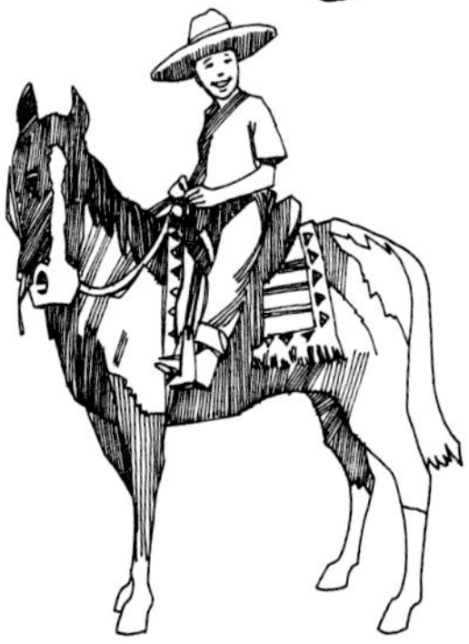

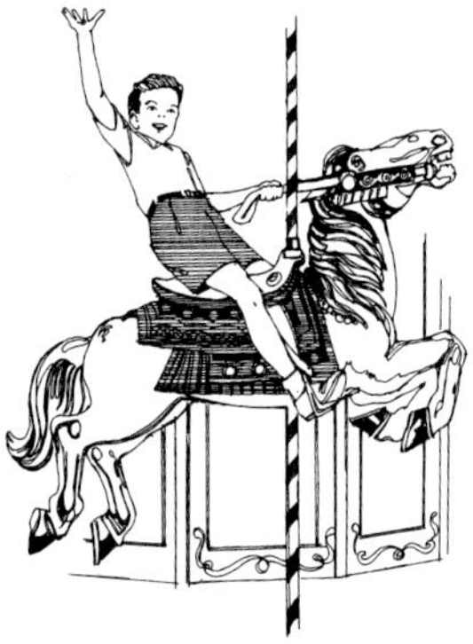

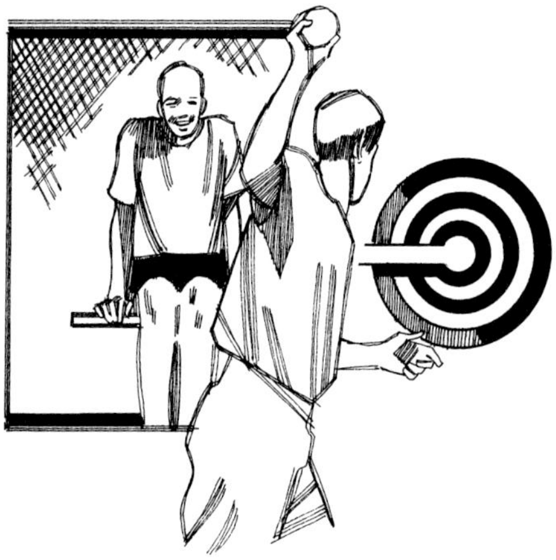

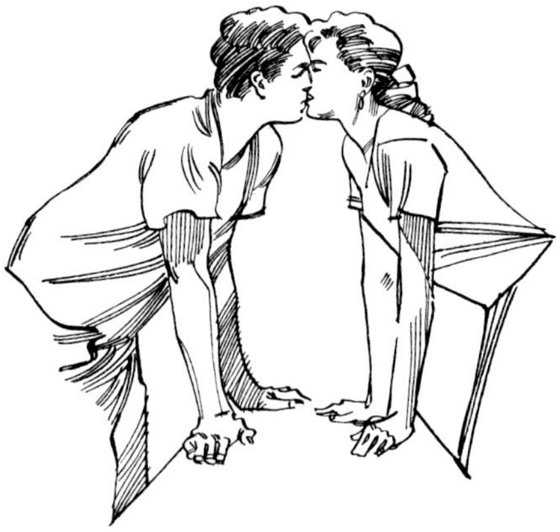

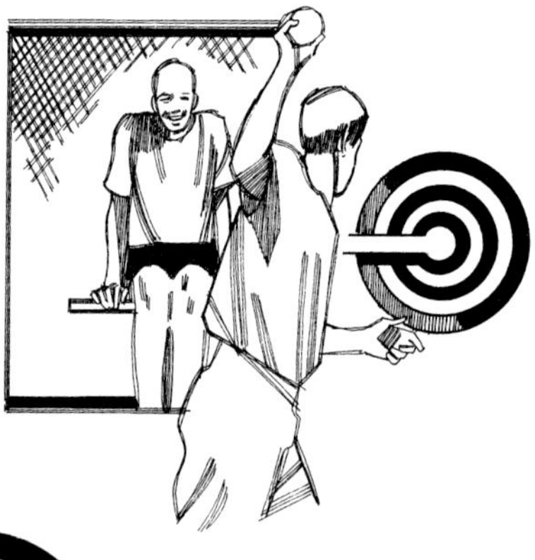

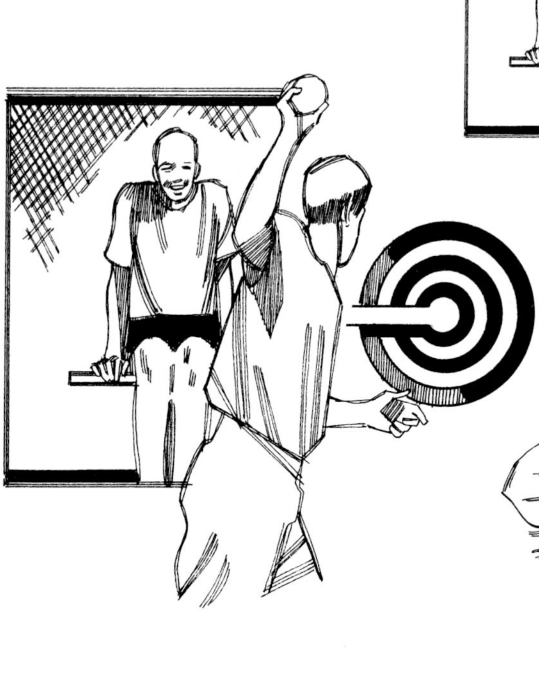

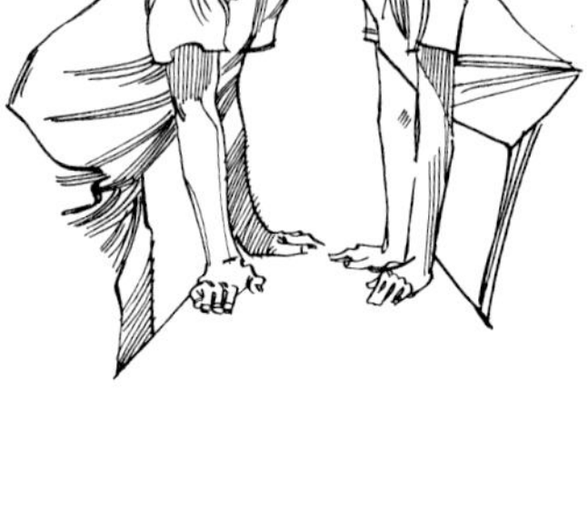

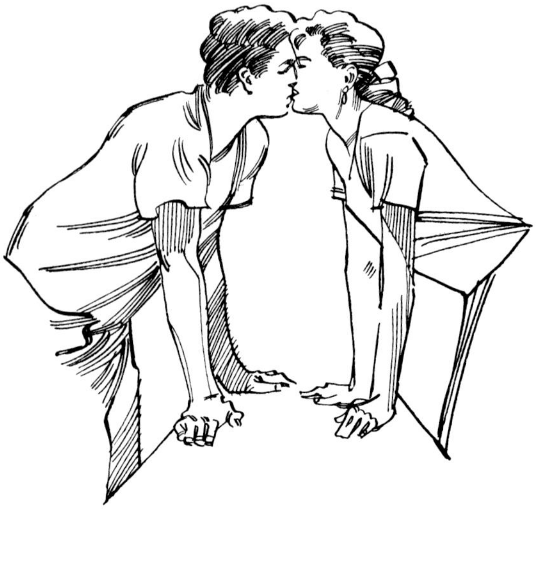

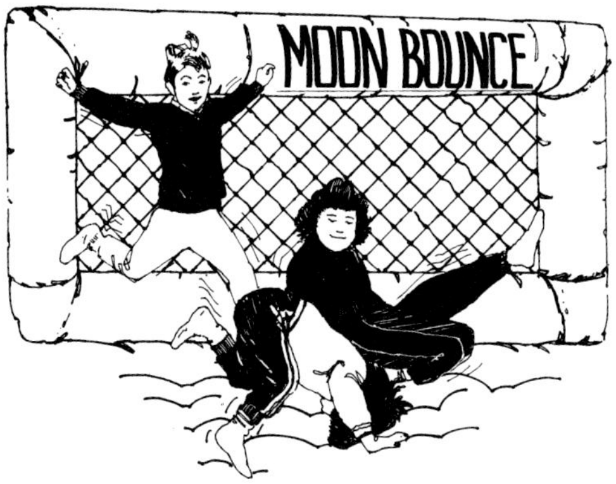
MOON BOUNCE

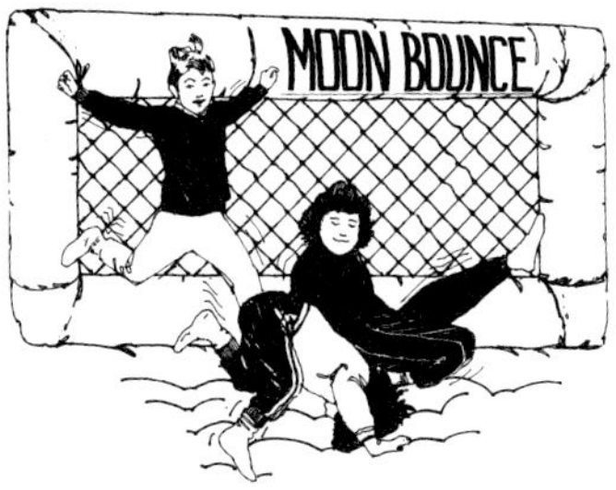
MOON BOUNCE

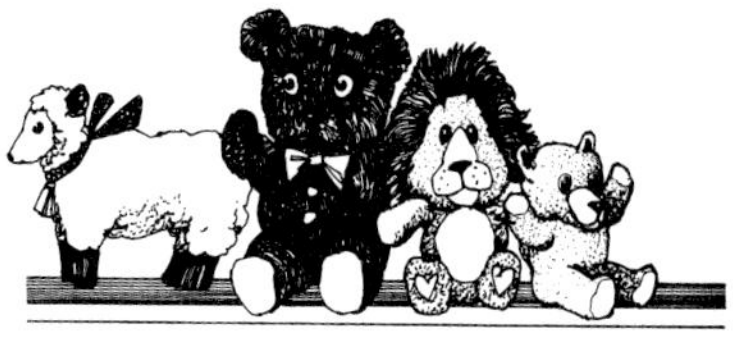

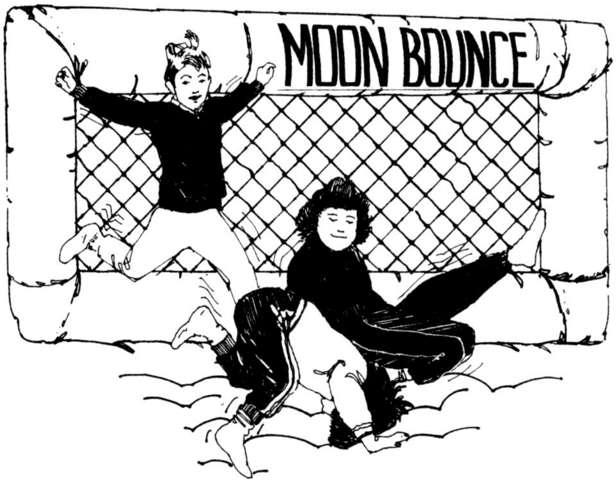
MOON BOUNCE

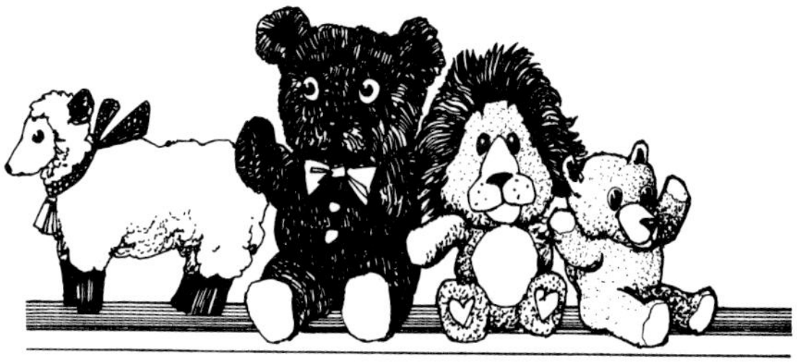

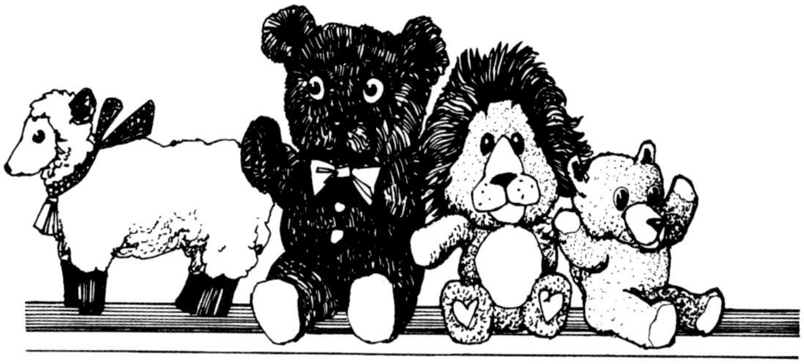

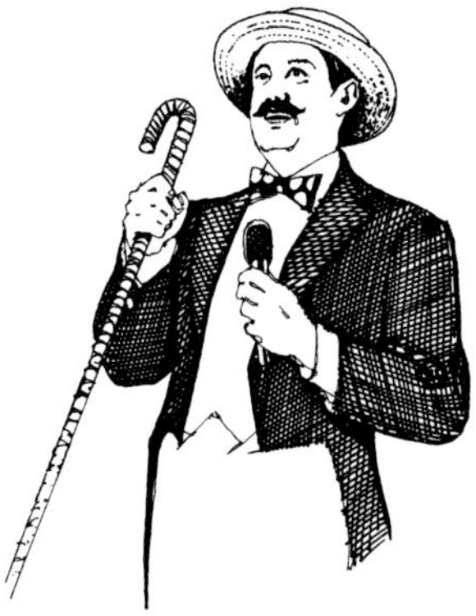

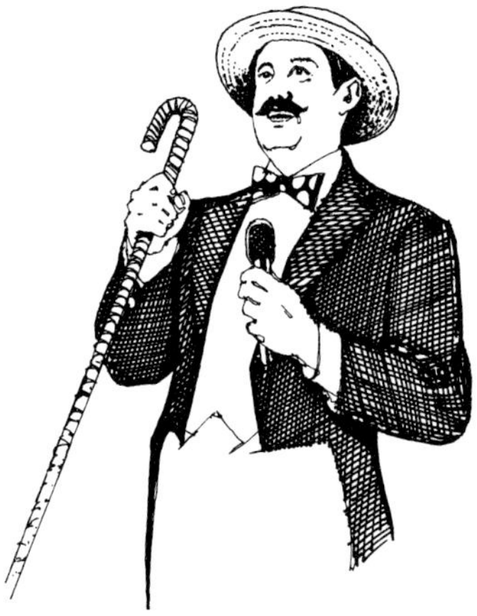

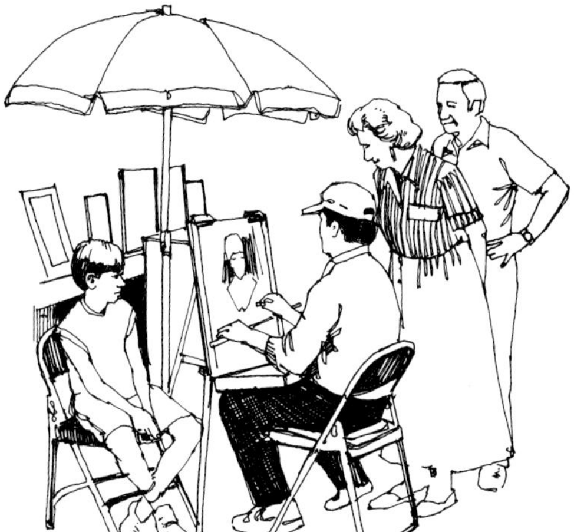

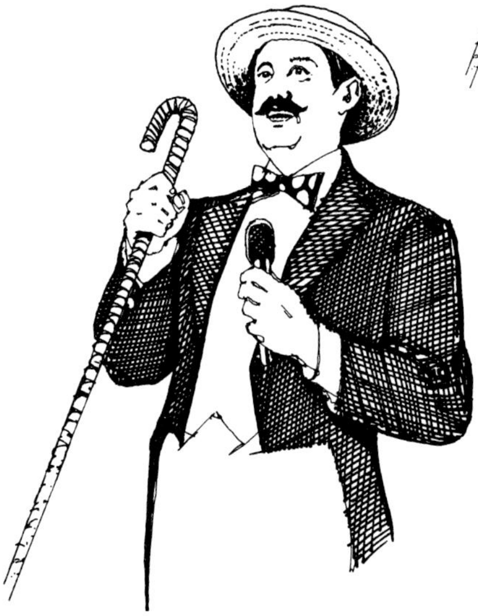

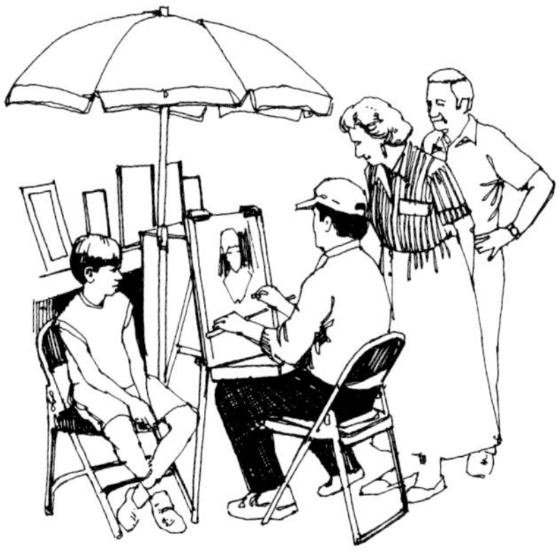

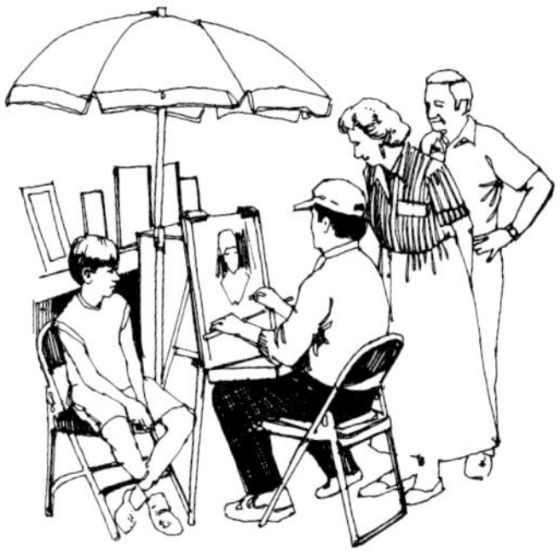

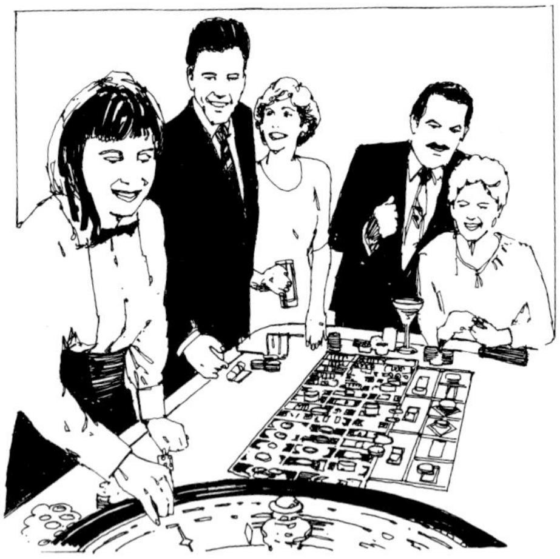

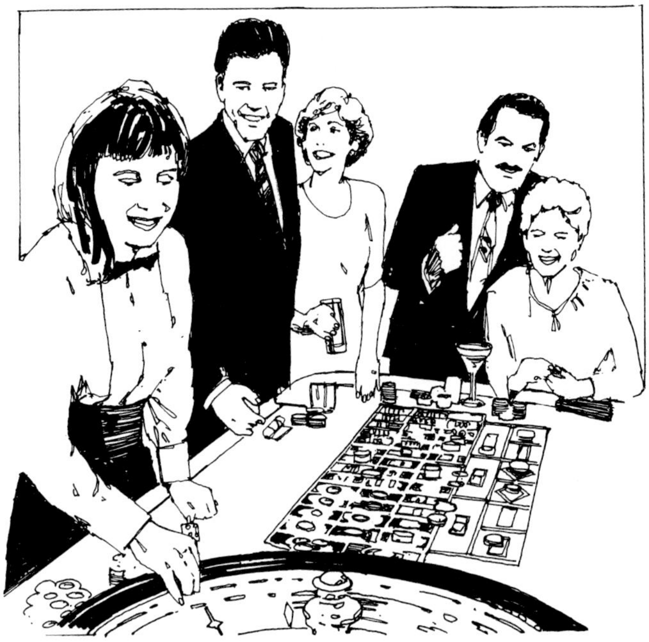

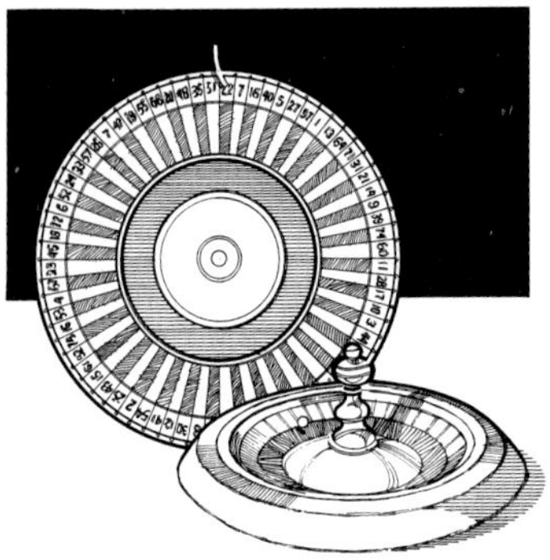

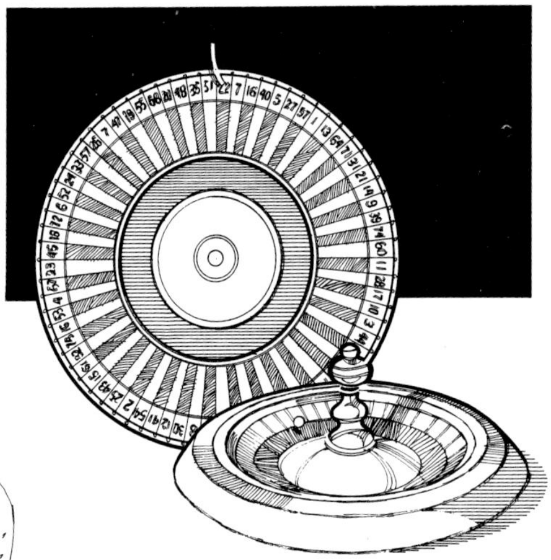

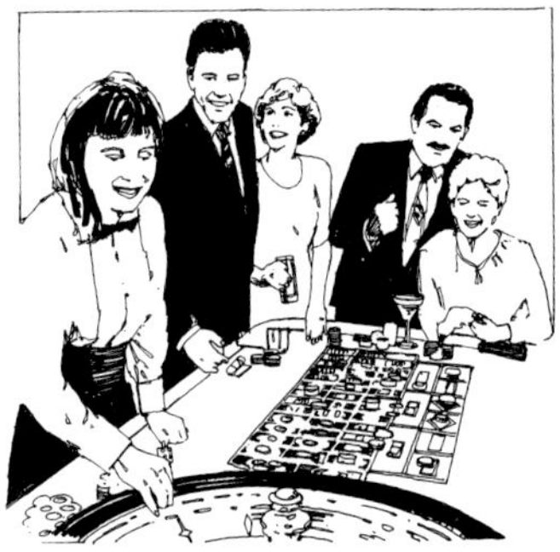

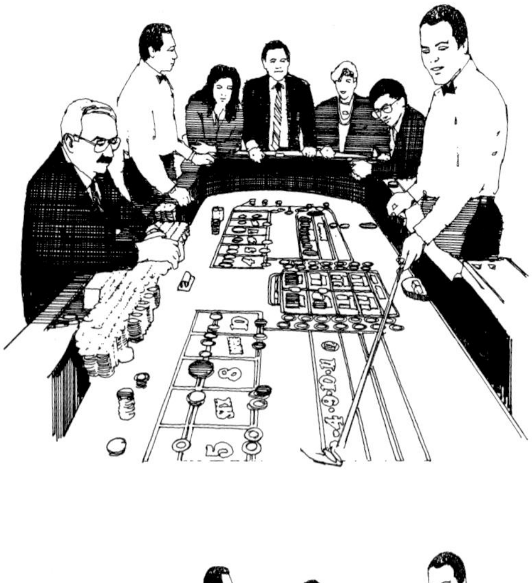

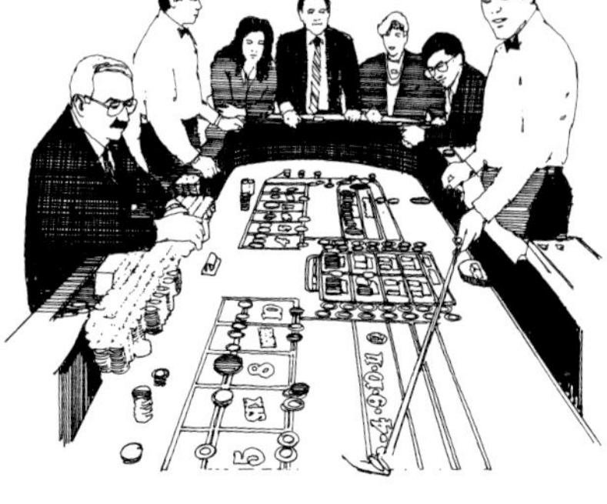

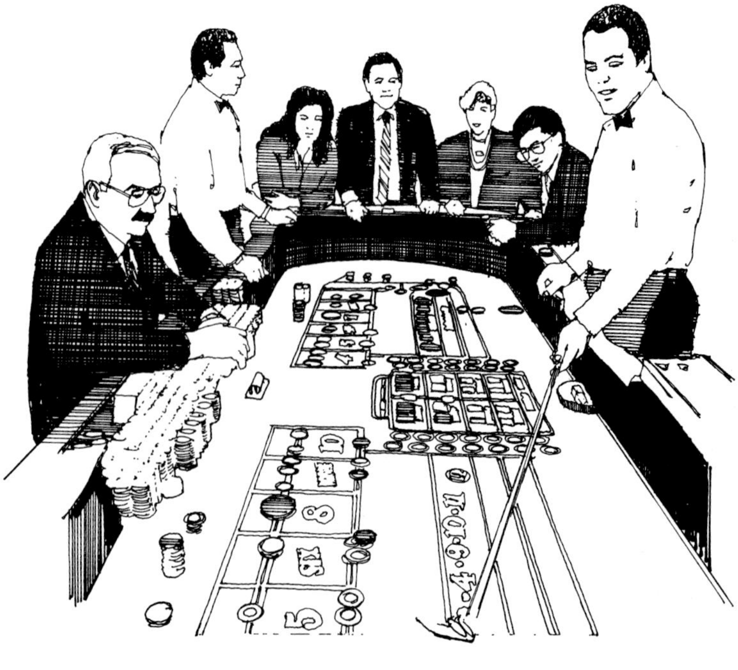

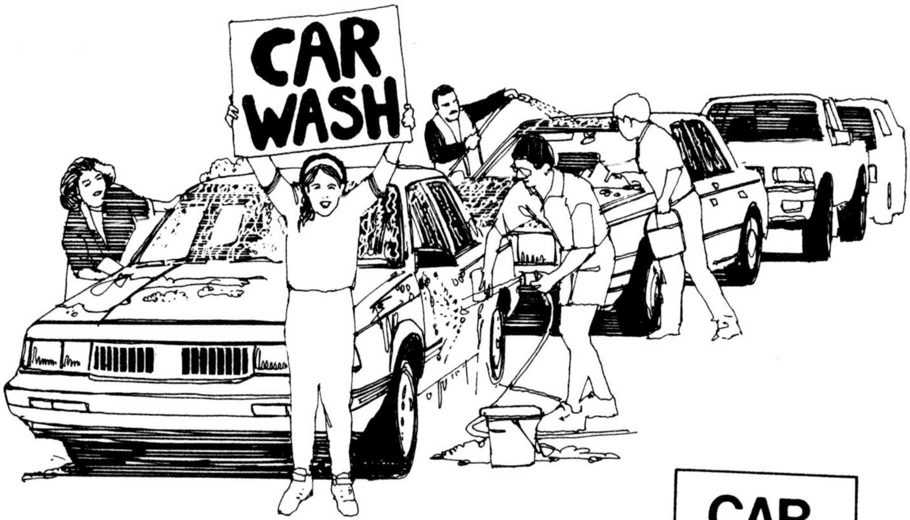
CAR
WASH

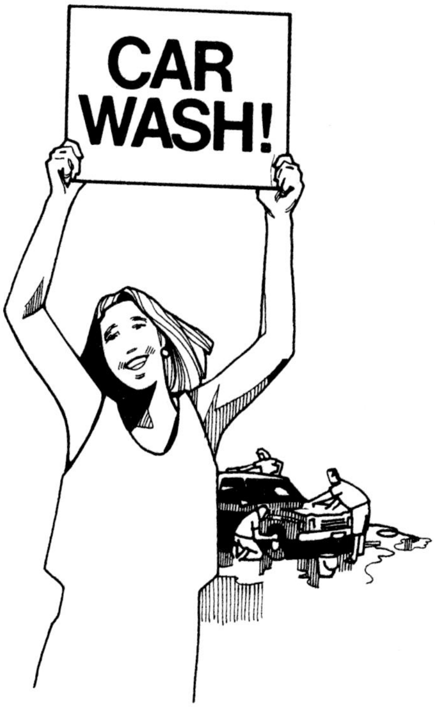
CAR
WASH!

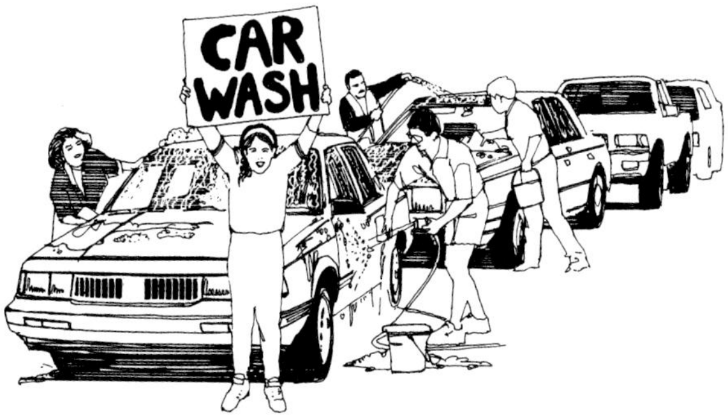
CAR
WASH

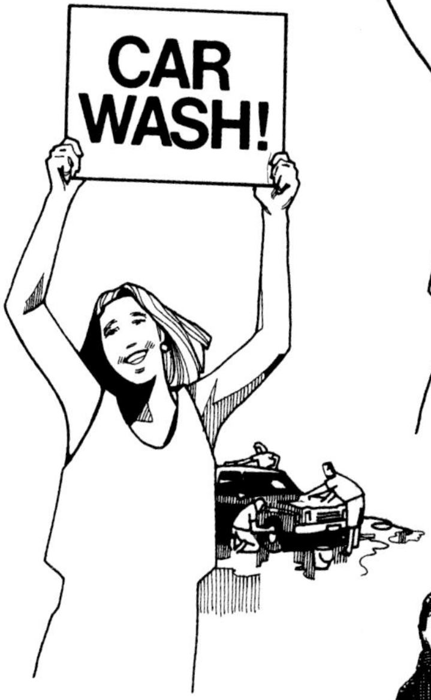
CAR
WASH!

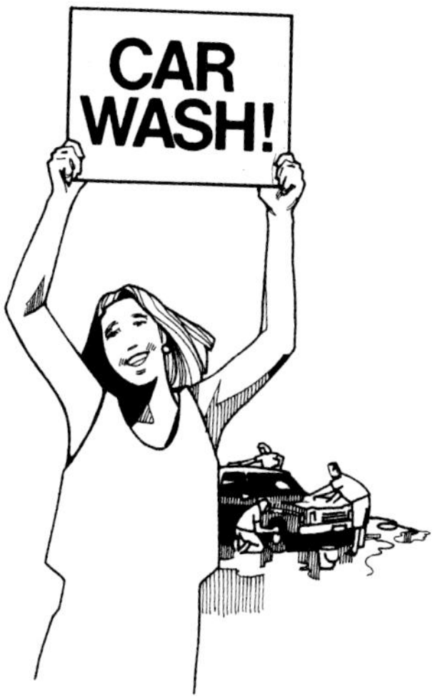
CAR
WASH!

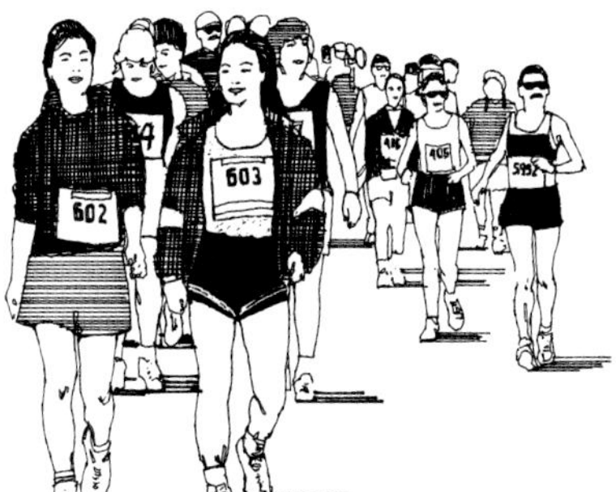
602
603

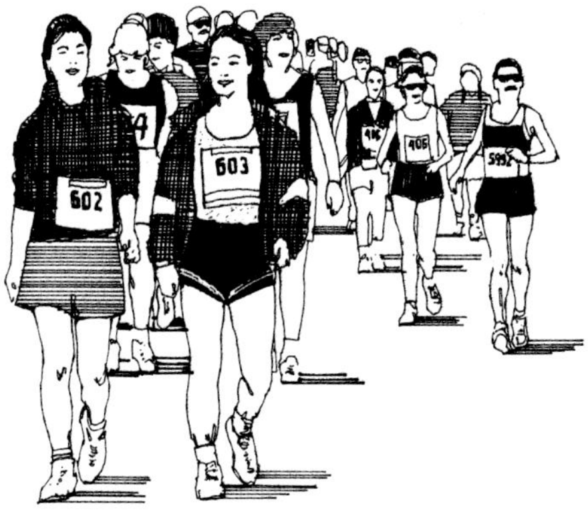
602
603

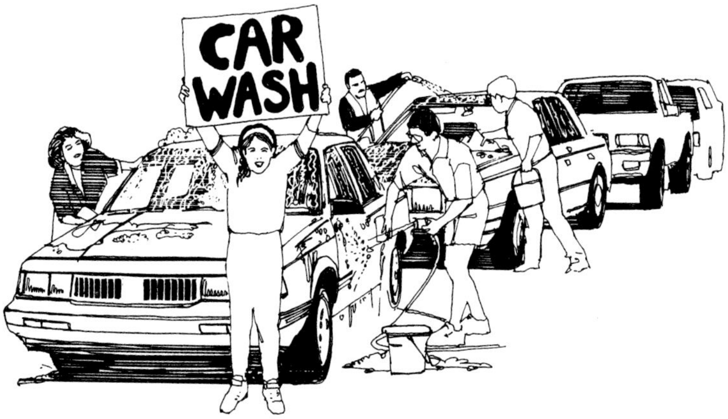
CAR
WASH

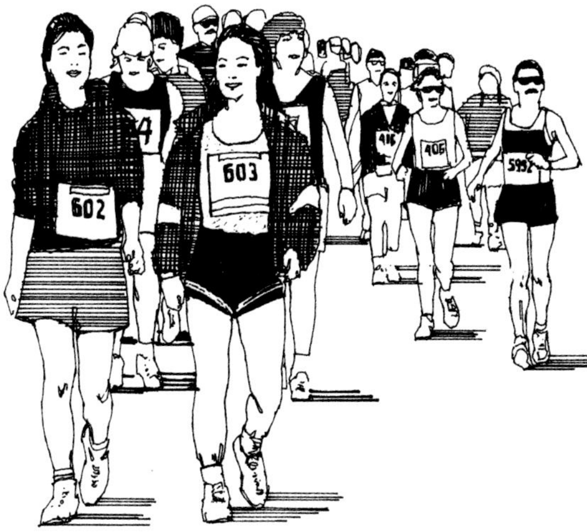
602
603
406

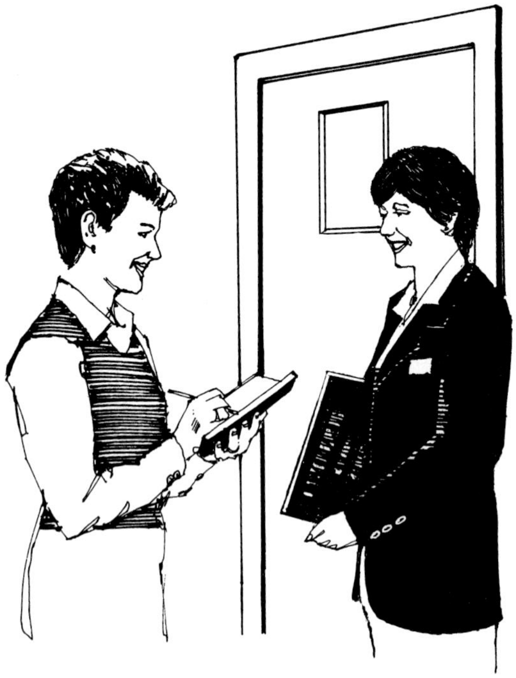

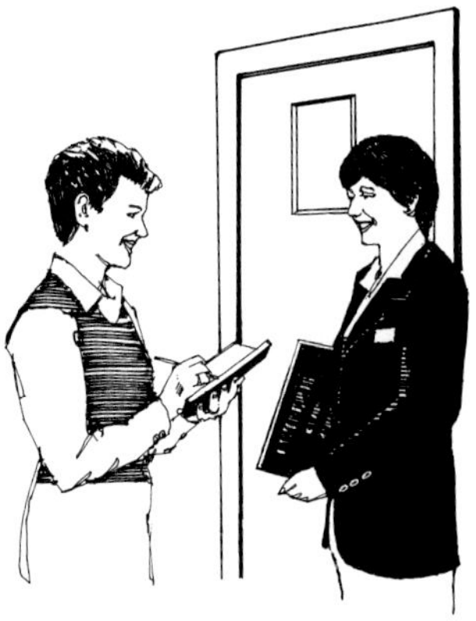

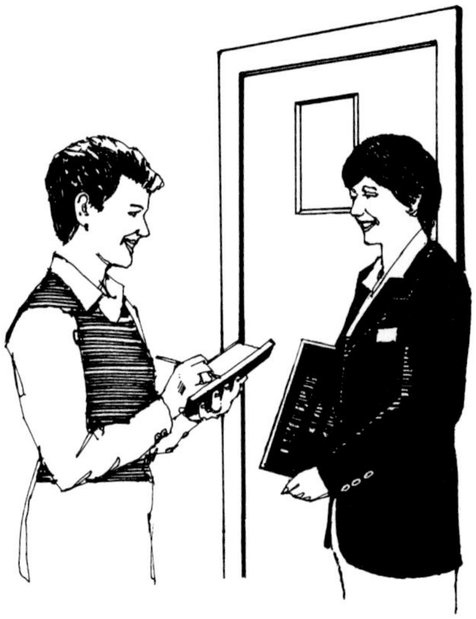

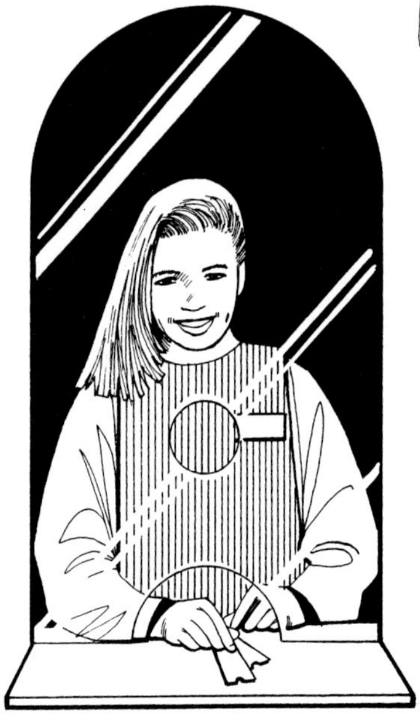

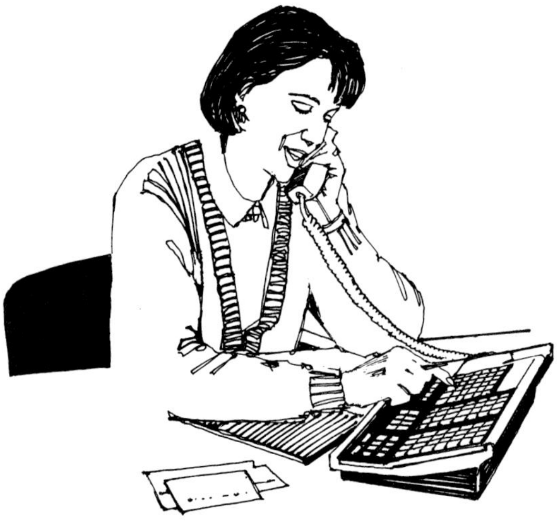

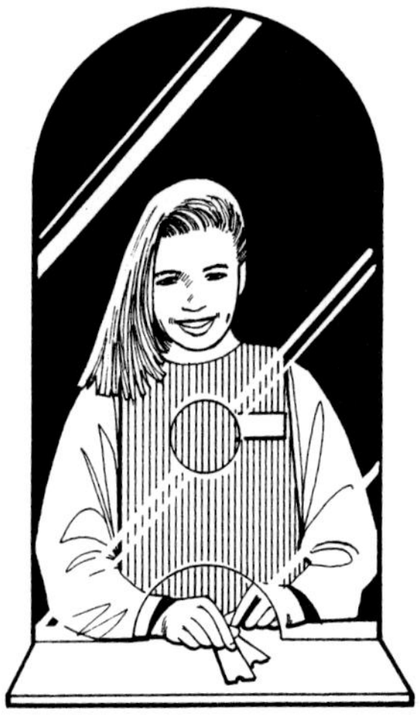

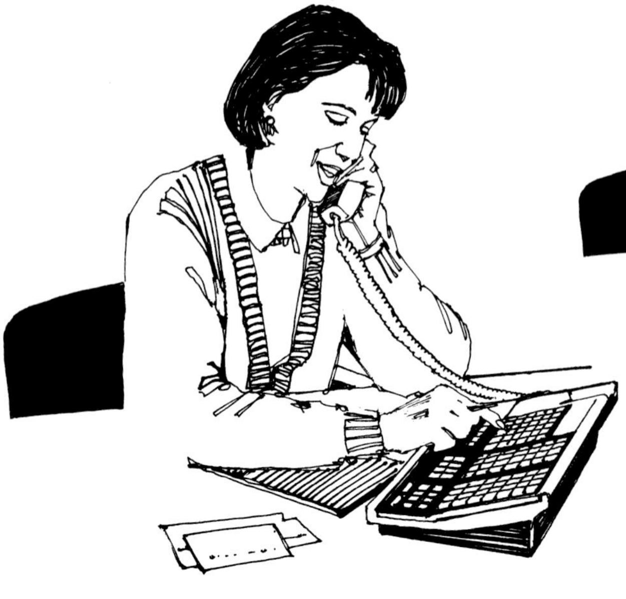

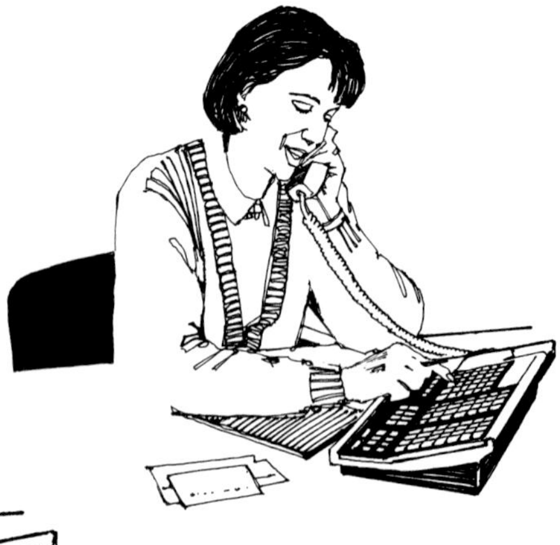

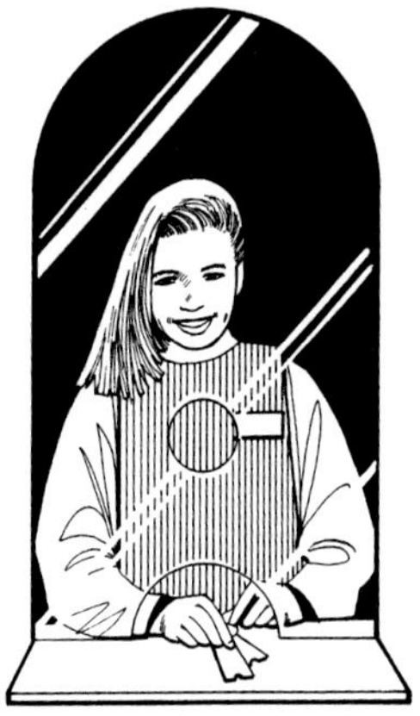

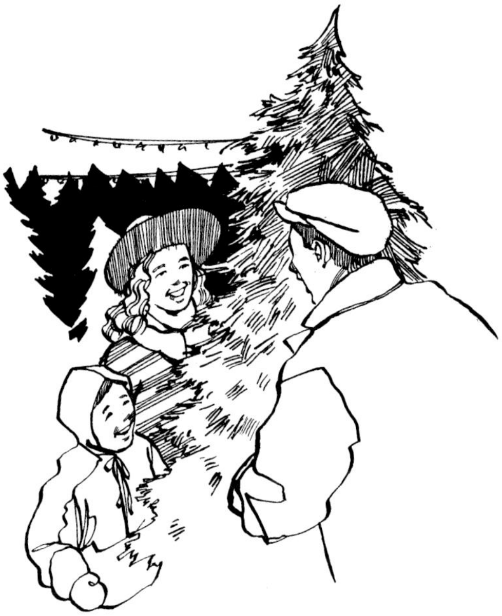

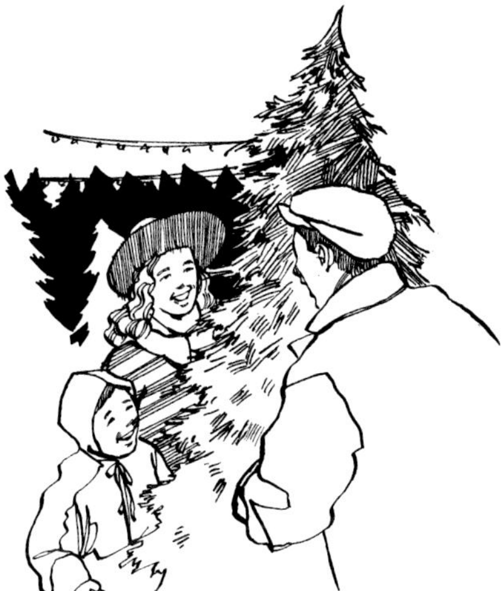

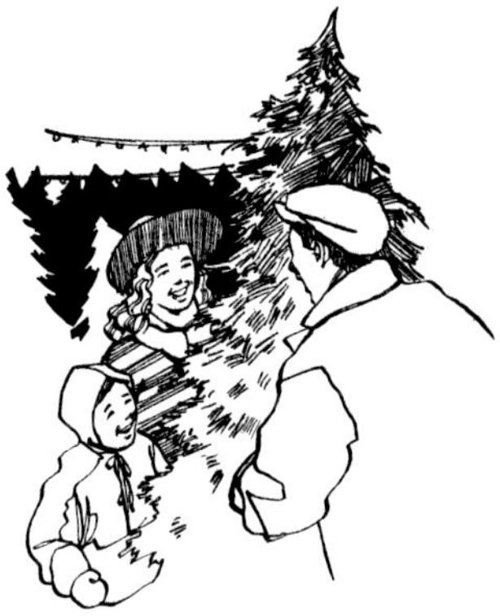

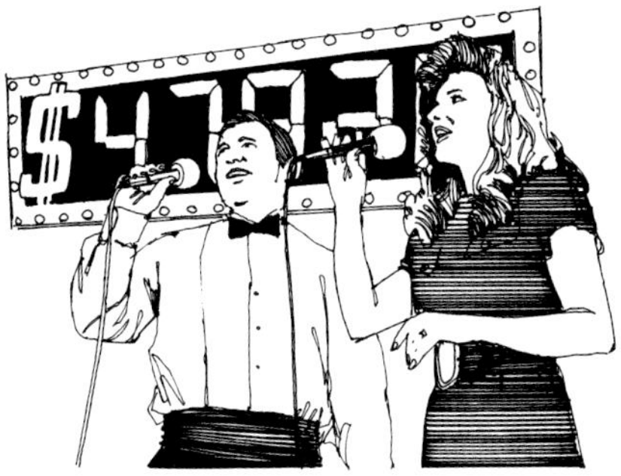

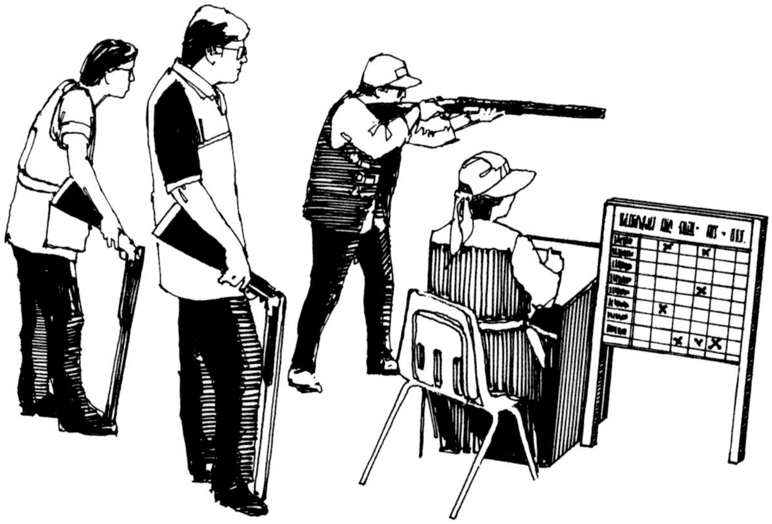

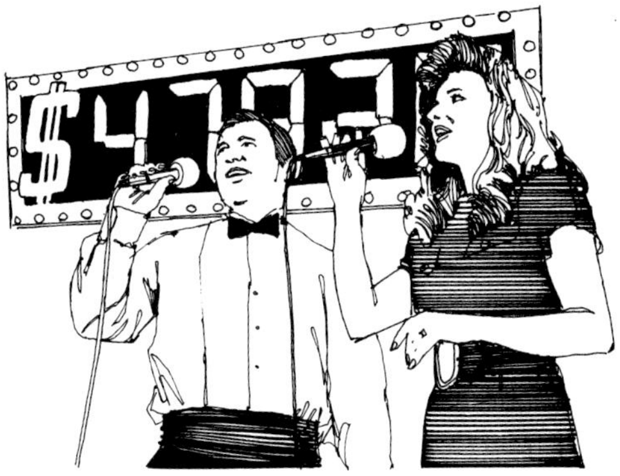

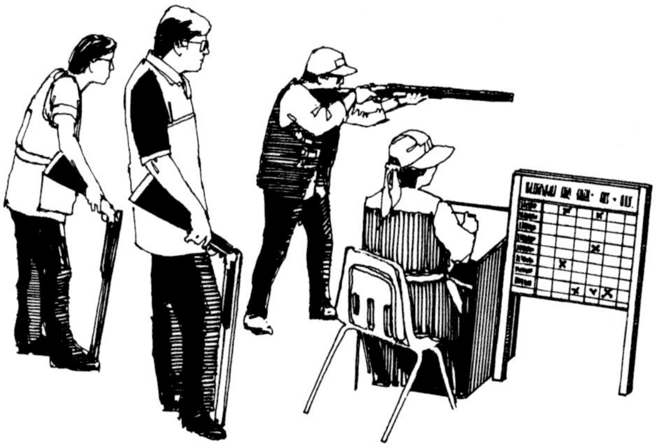

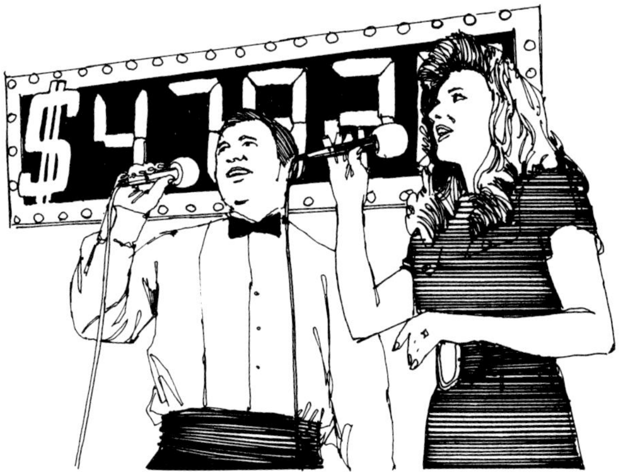

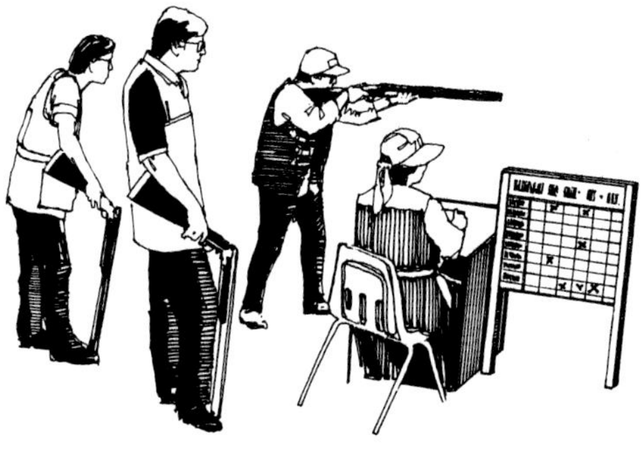

■ Money Makers

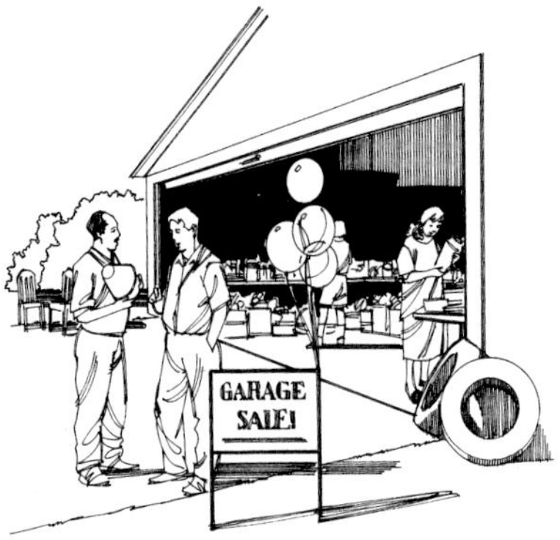

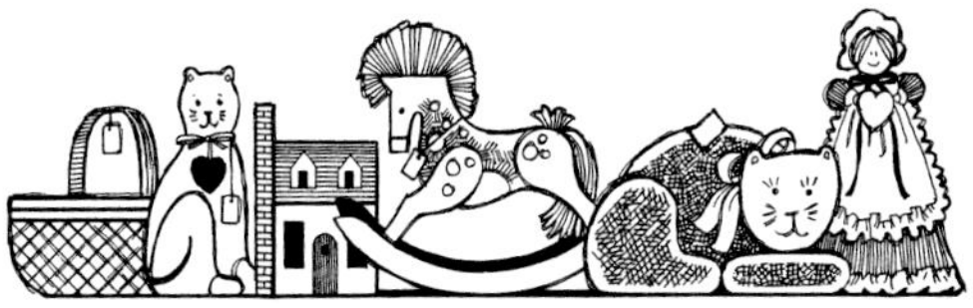

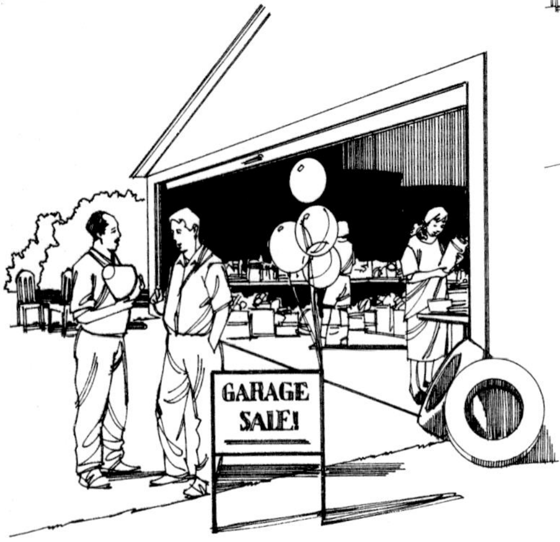

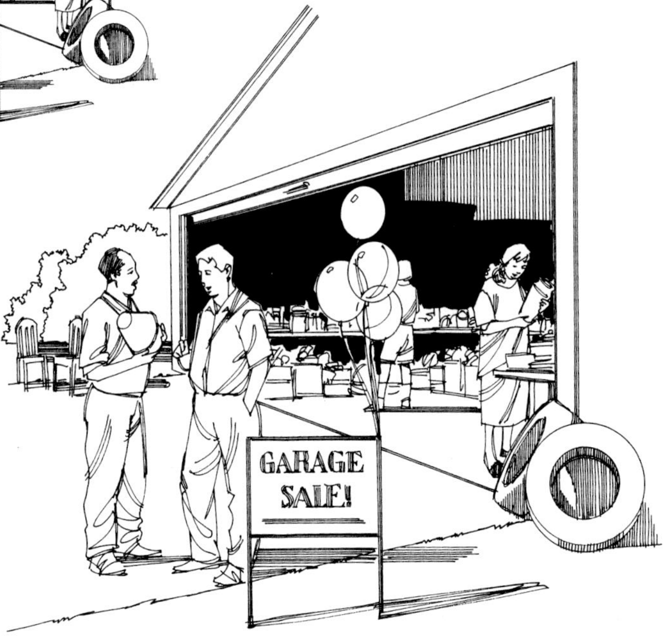

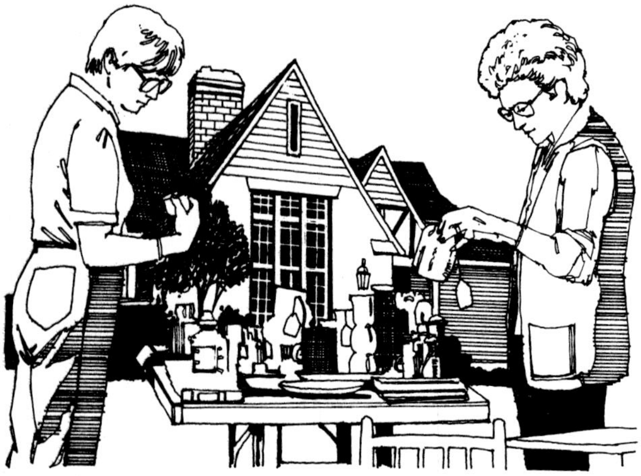

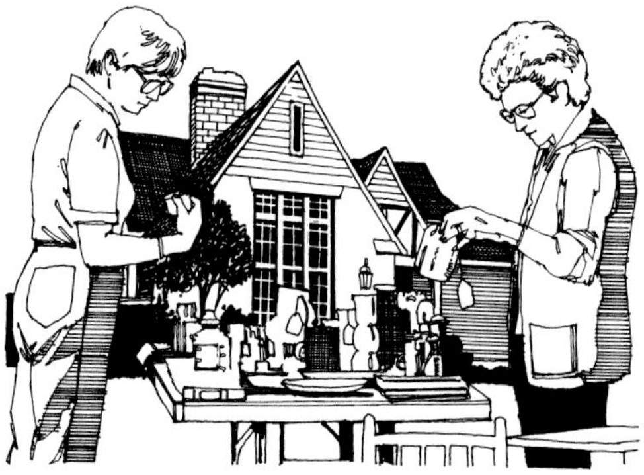

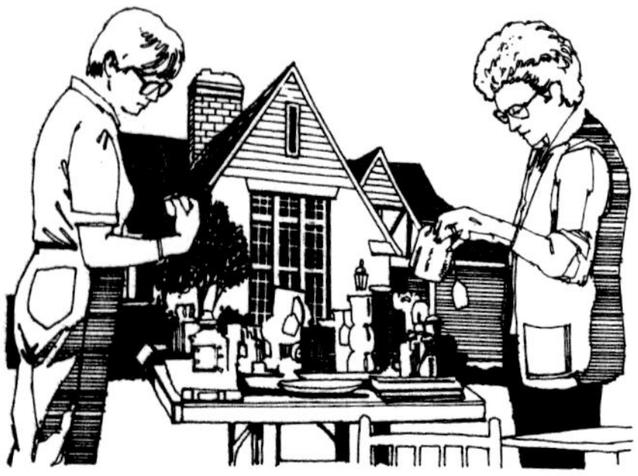

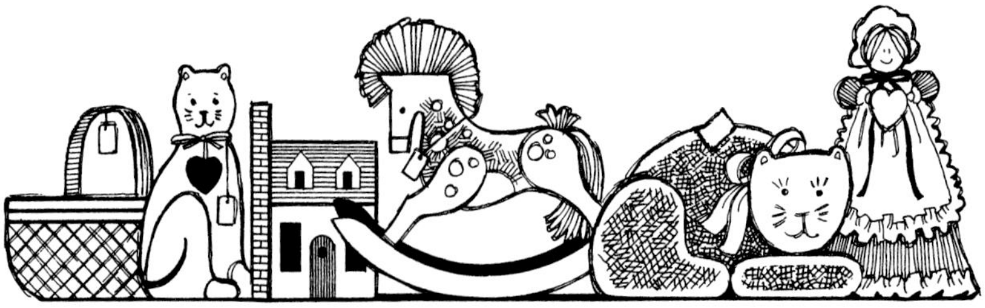

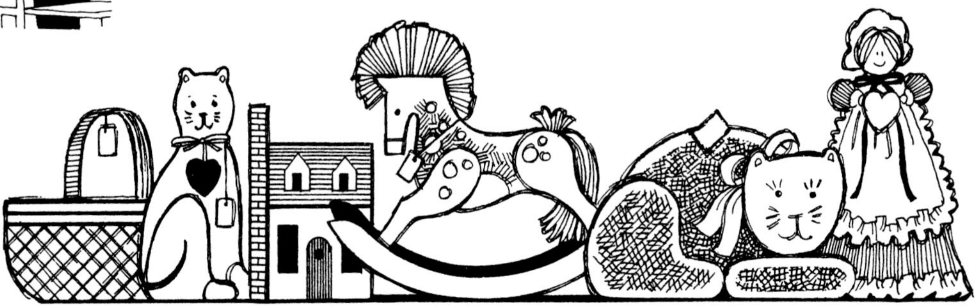

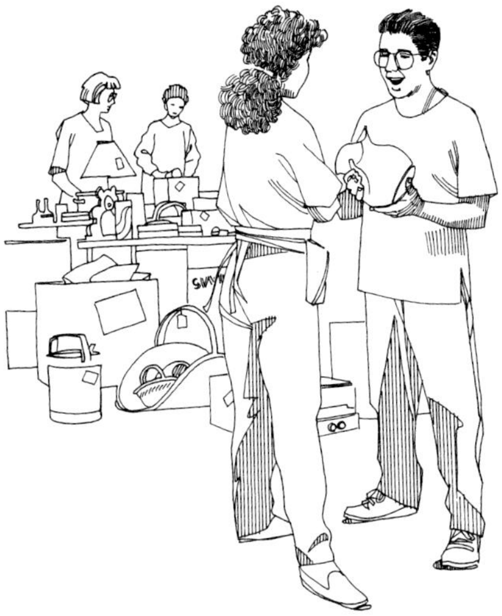

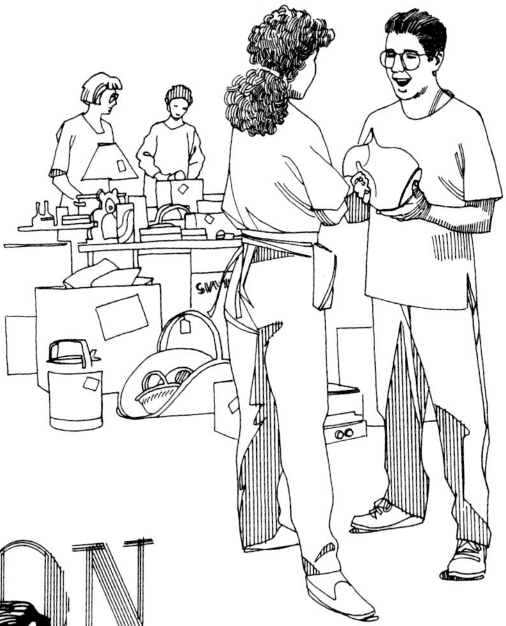

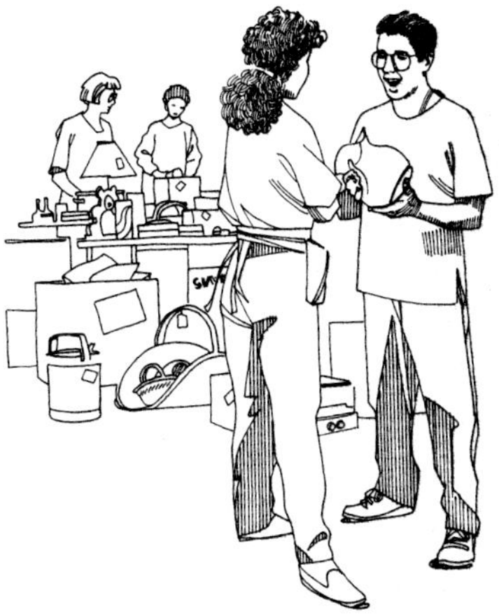

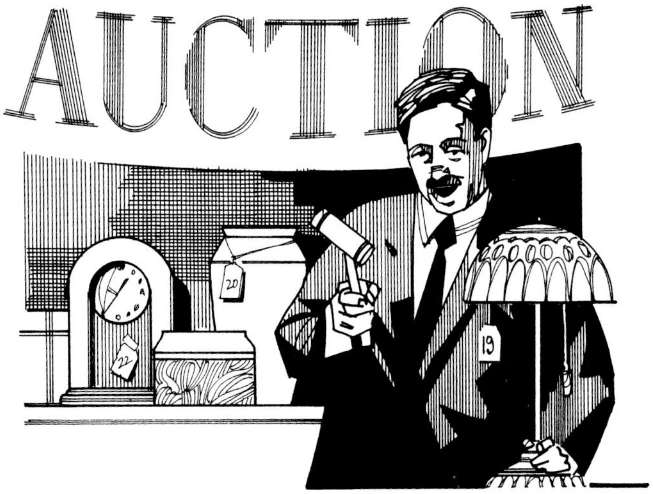
AUCTION

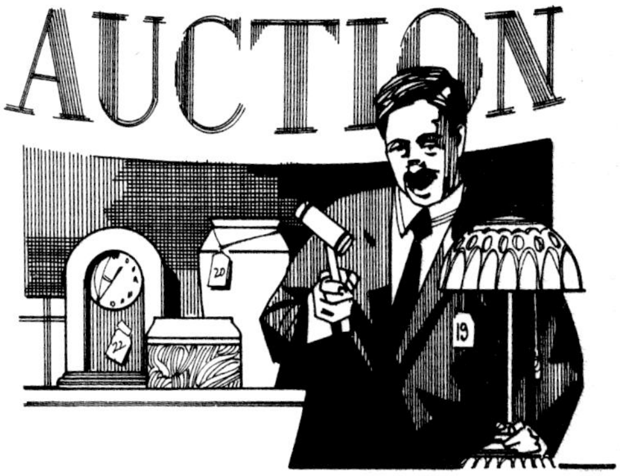
AUCTION

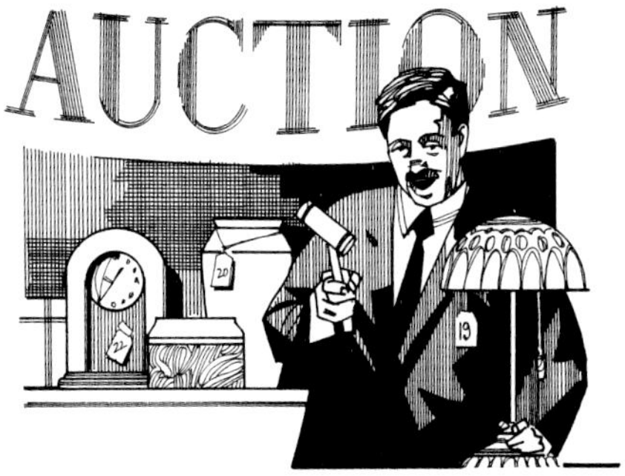
AUCTION

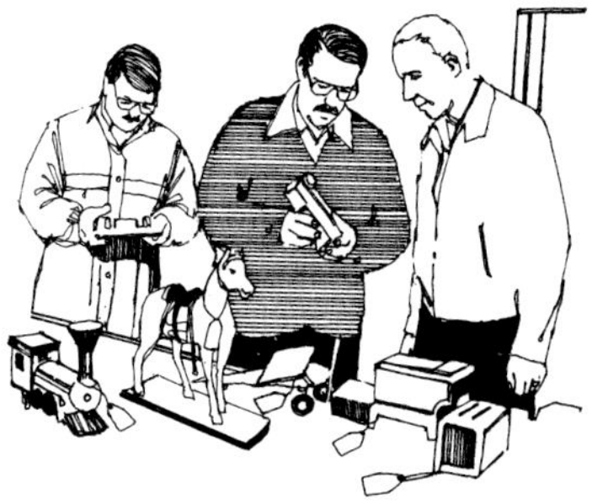

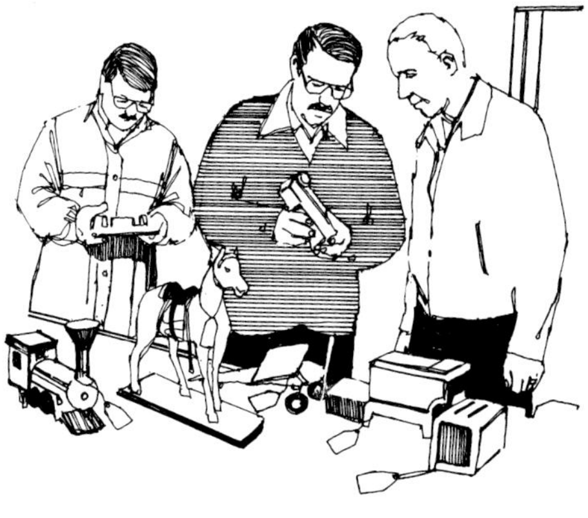

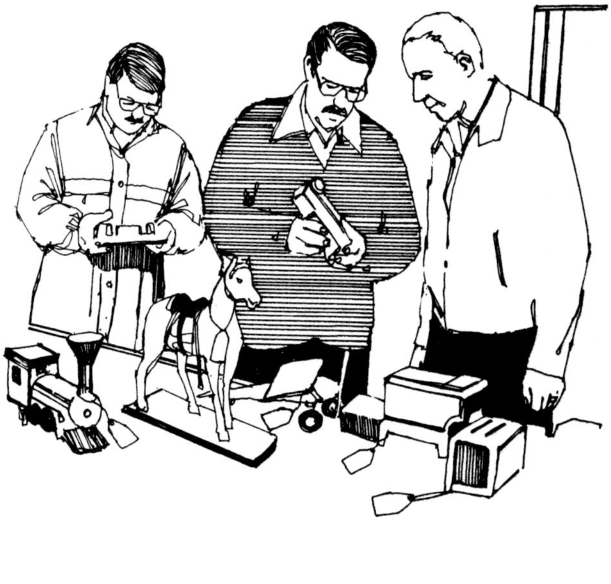

■ Money Makers

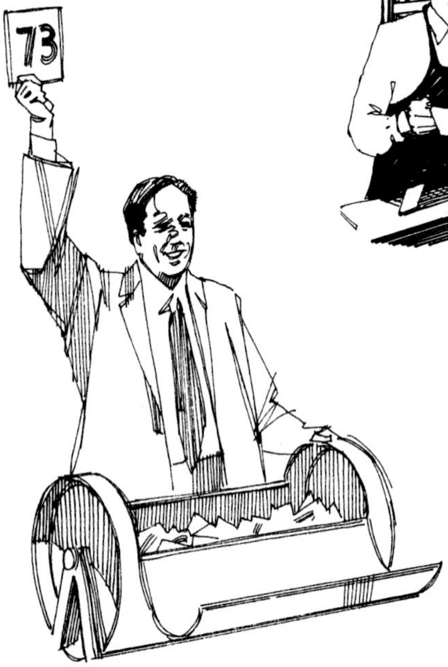

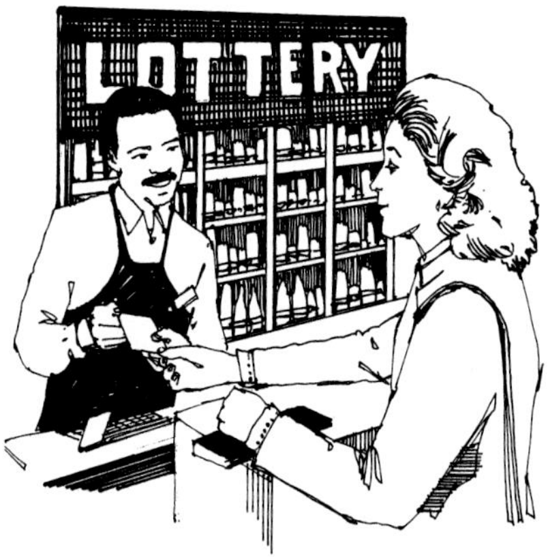

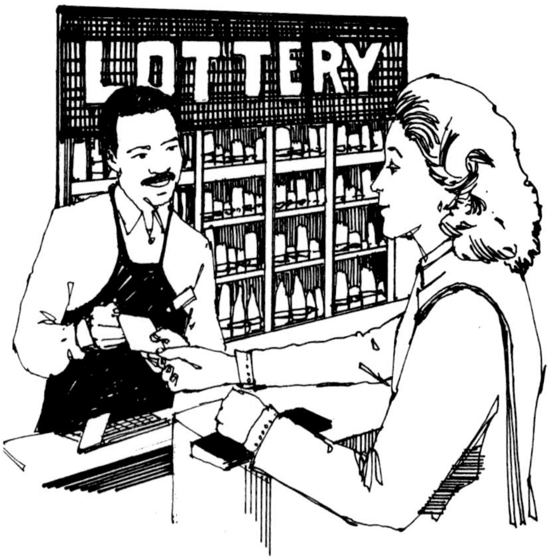

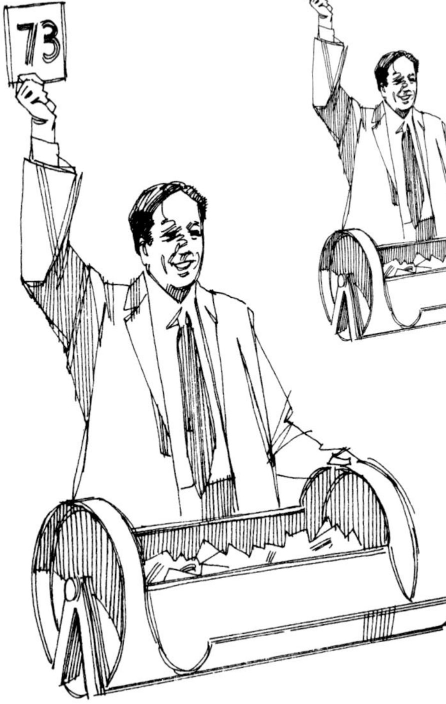

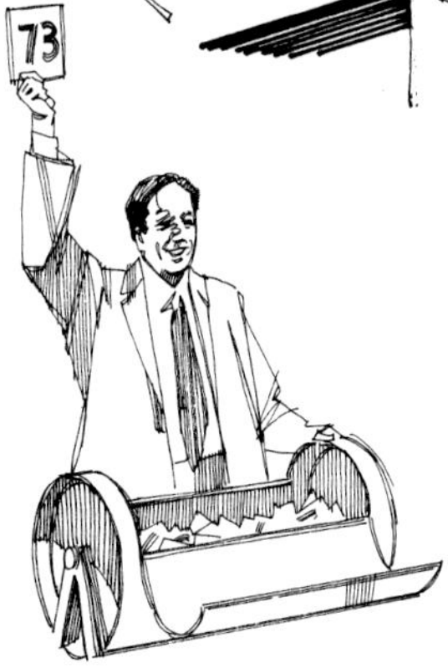

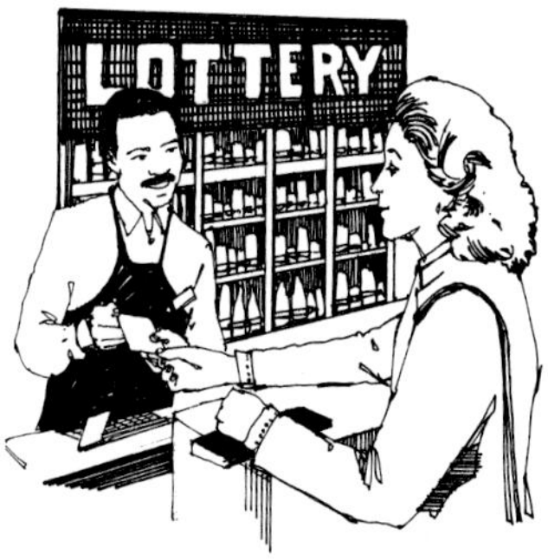

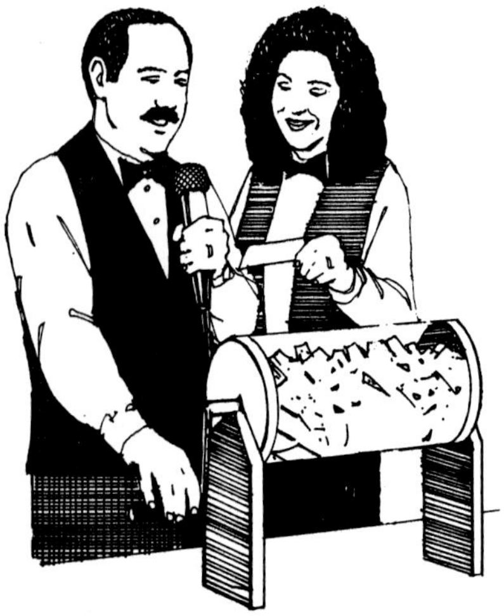

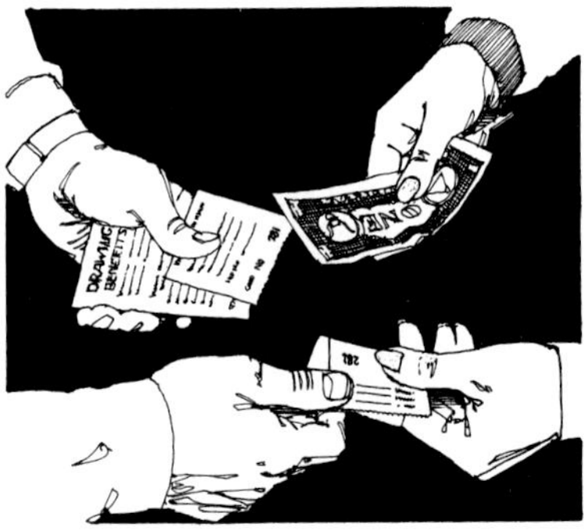

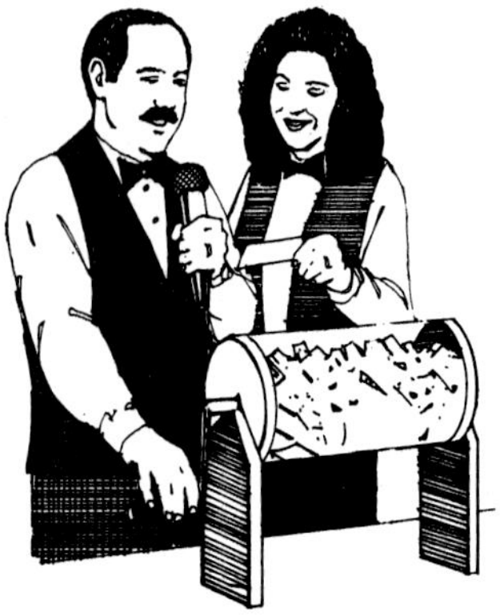

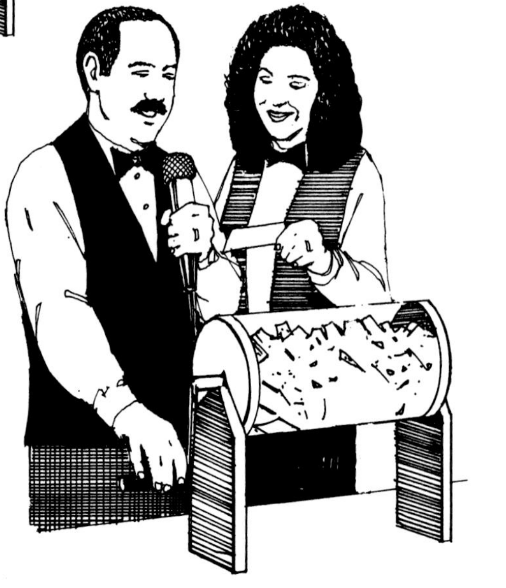

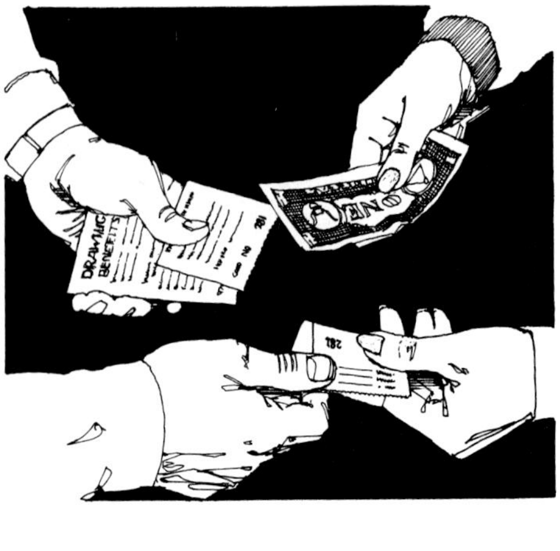

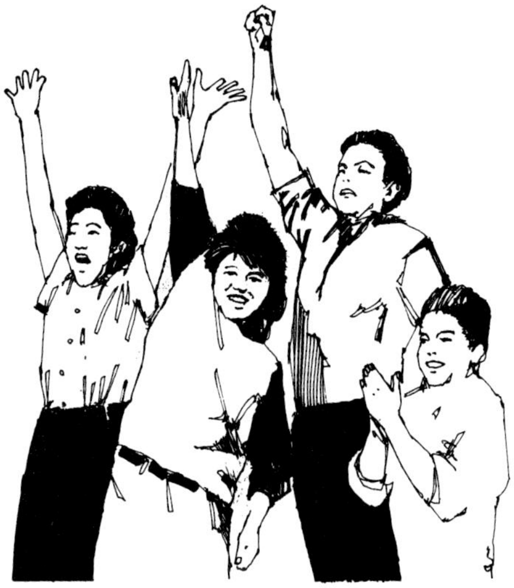

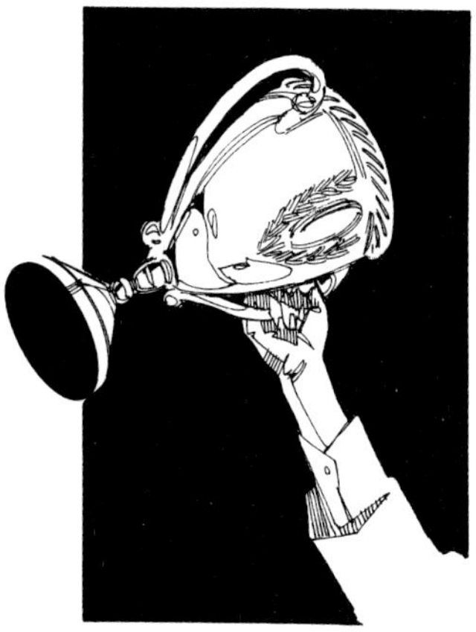

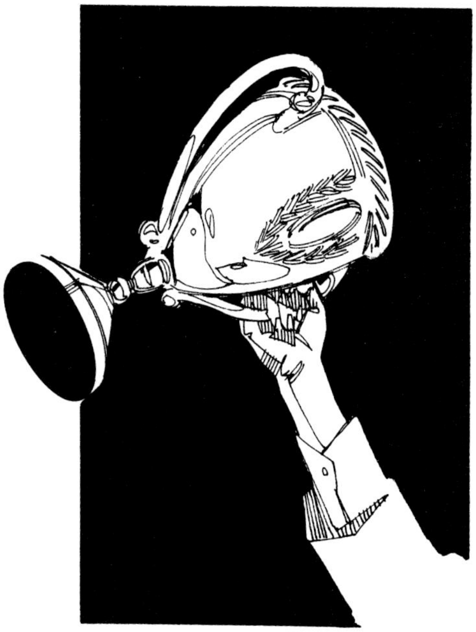

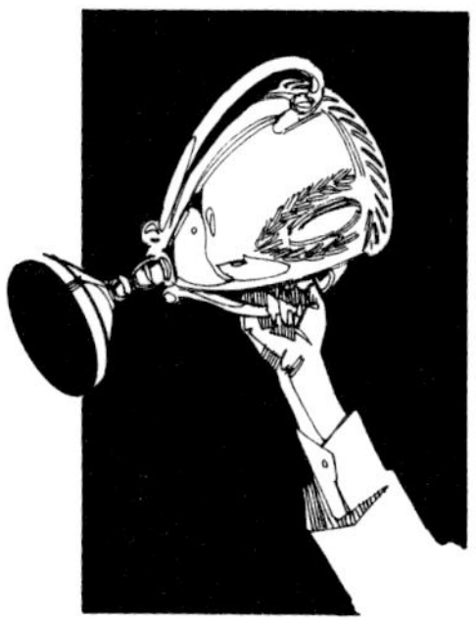

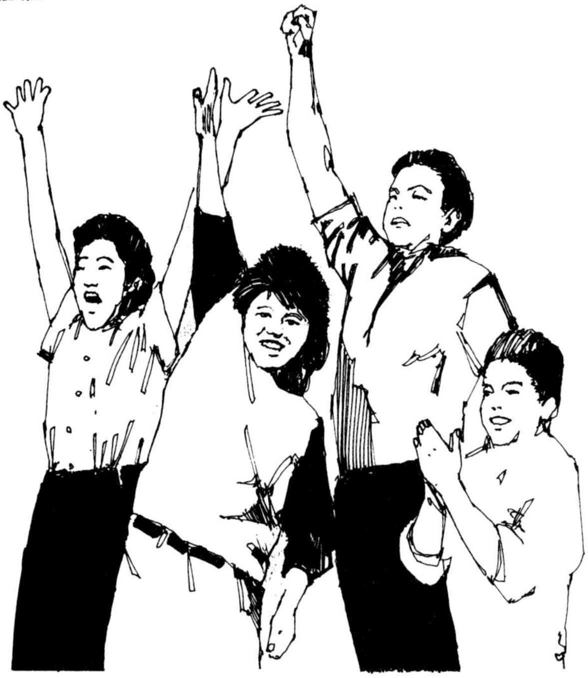

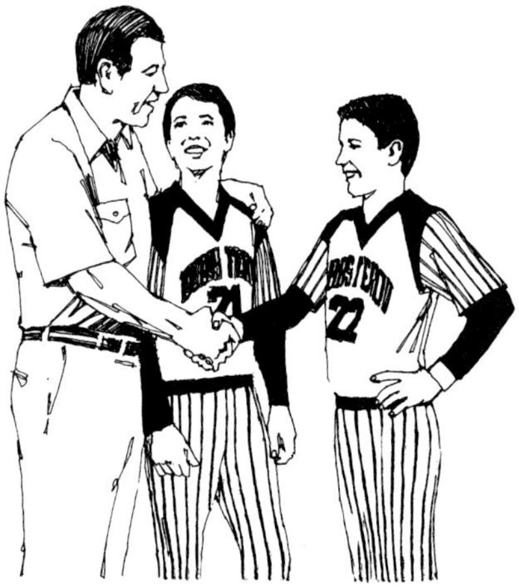

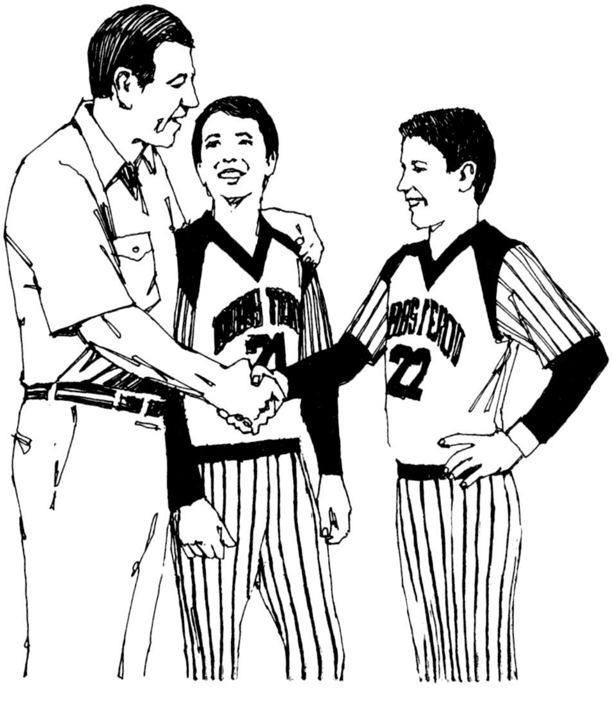

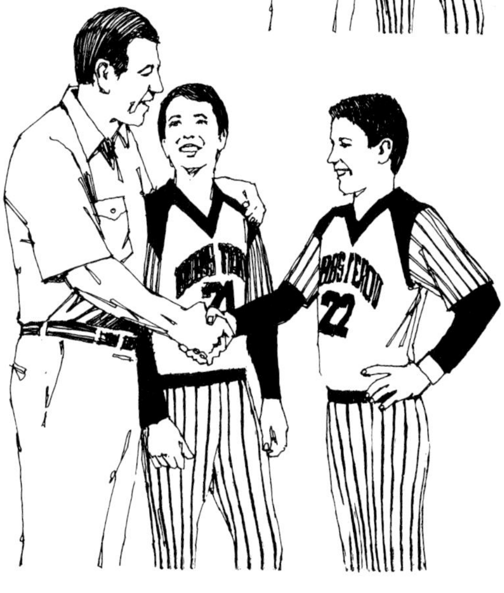

Happy Results

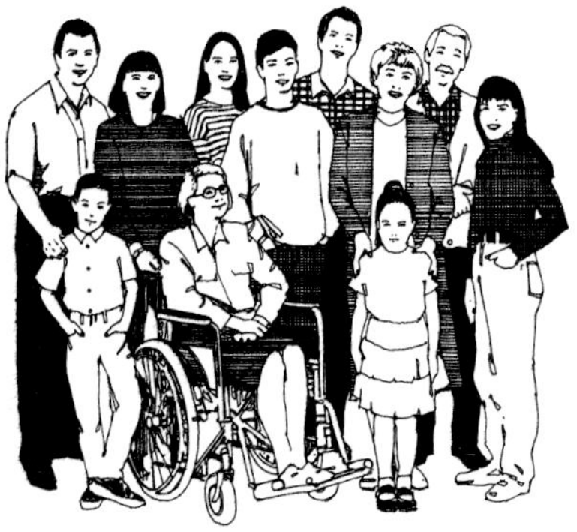

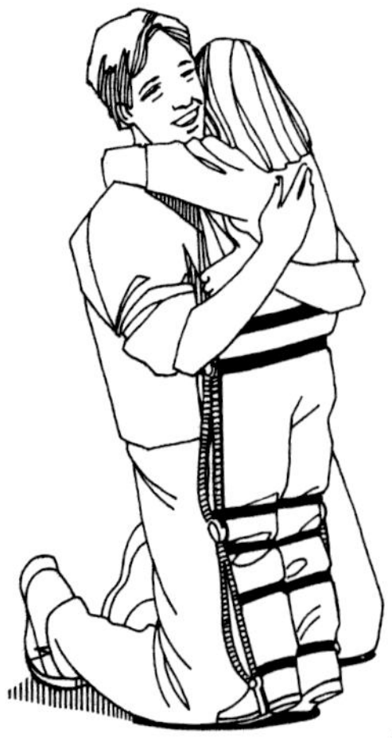

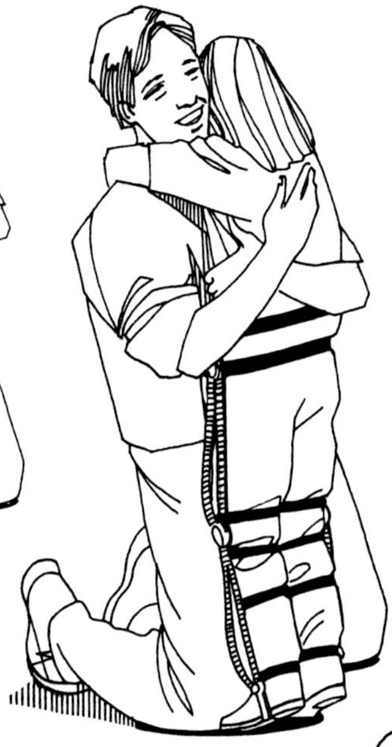

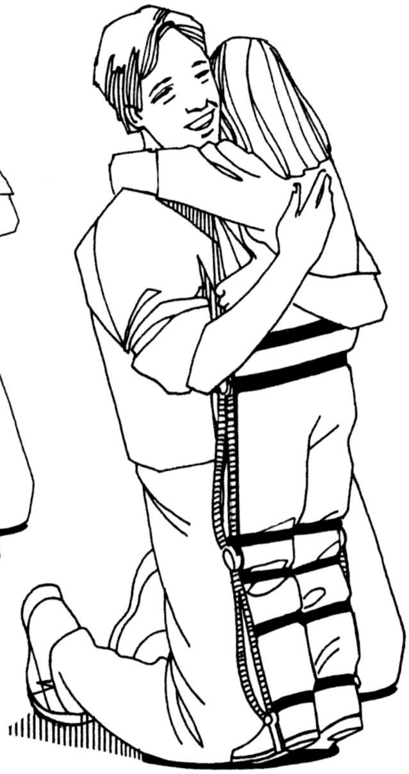

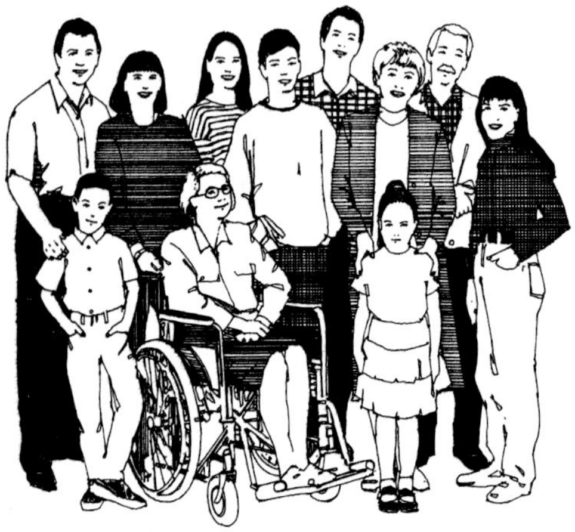

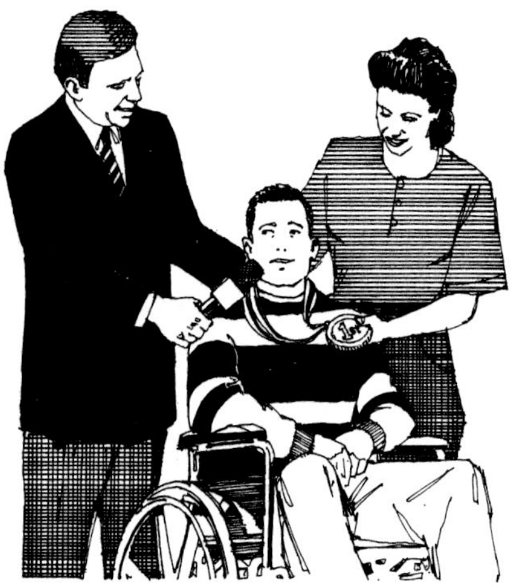

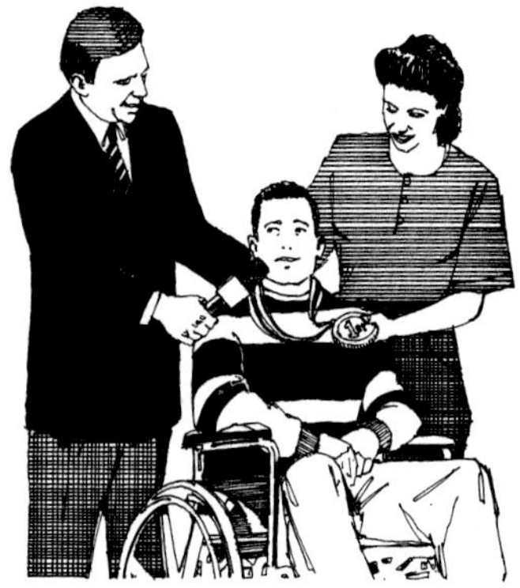

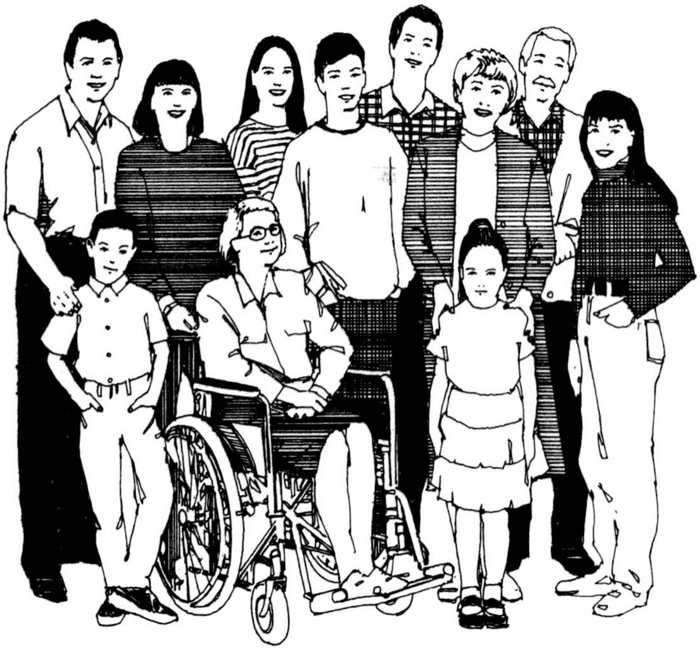

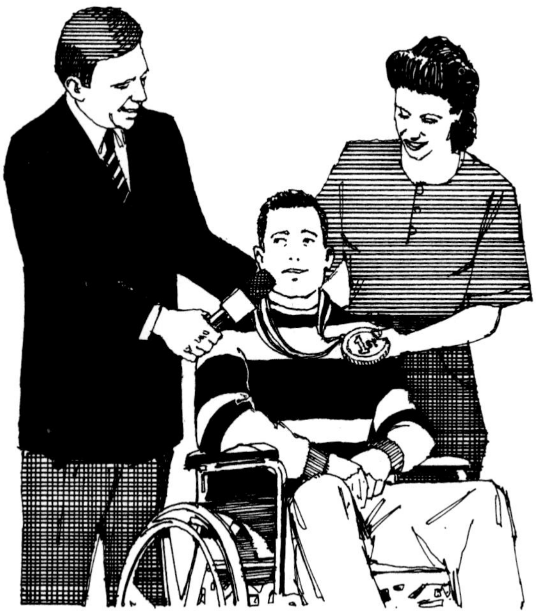

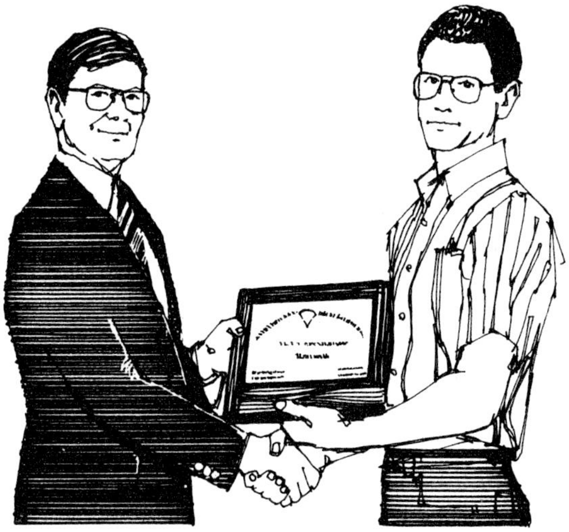

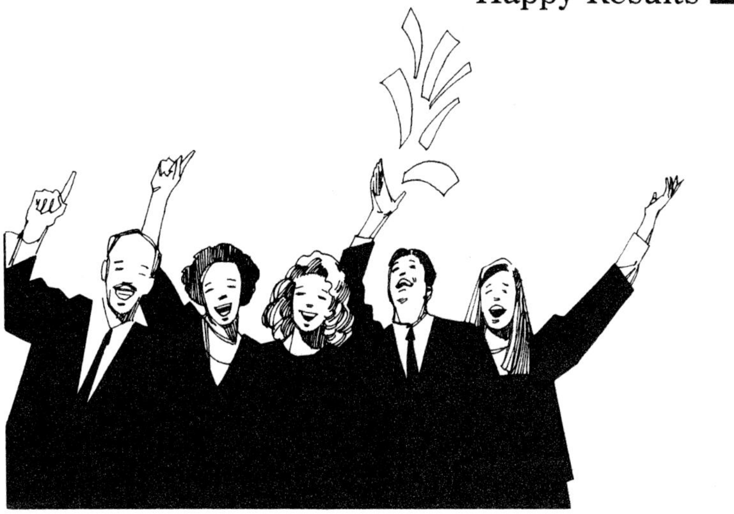

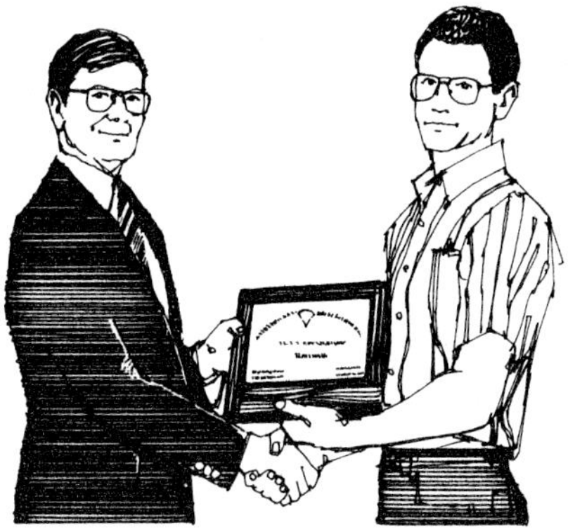

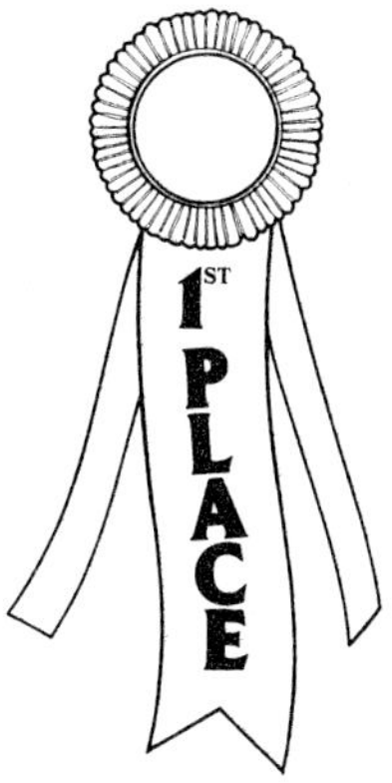
1ST
PLACE

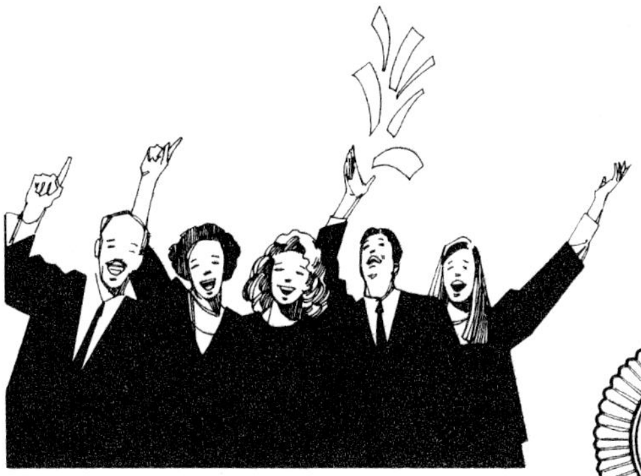

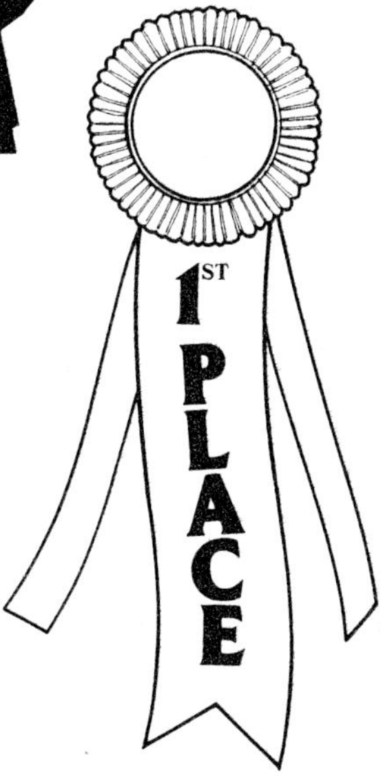
1ST
PLACE

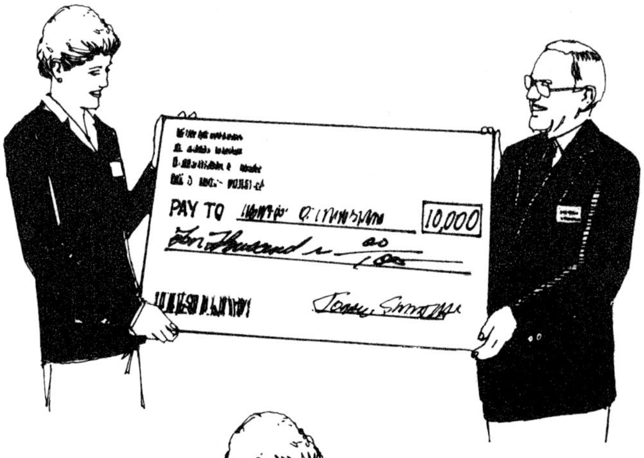
PAY TO
10,000

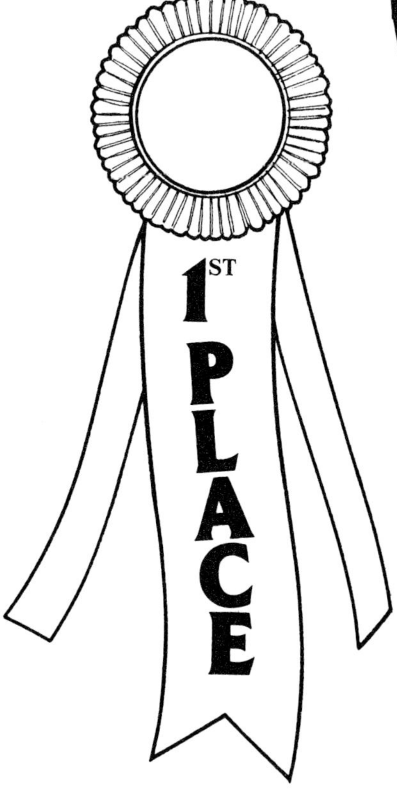
1ST
PLACE

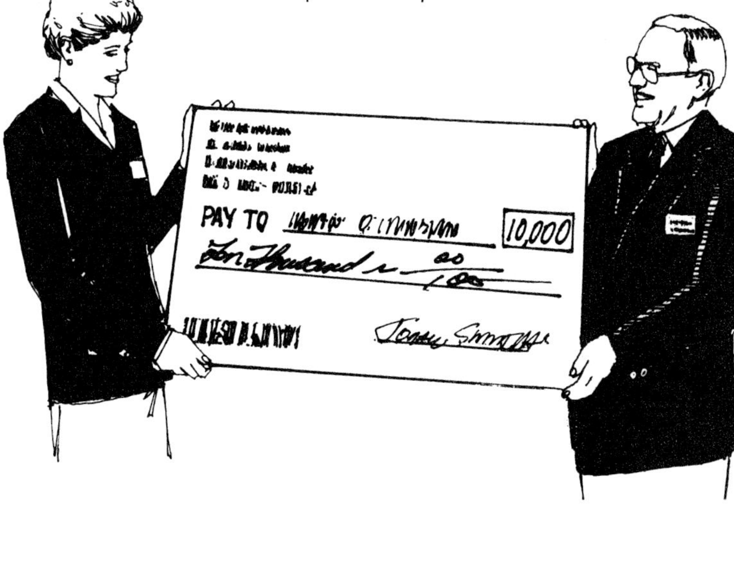
PAY TO
10,000

Happy Results

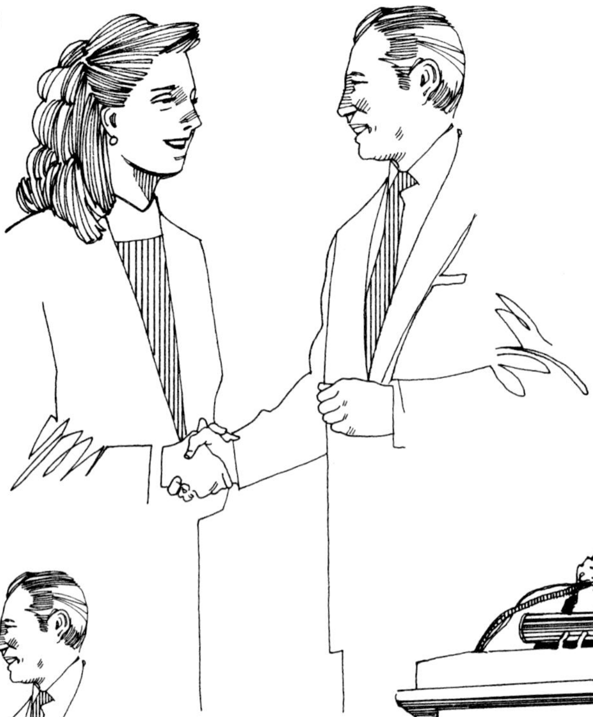

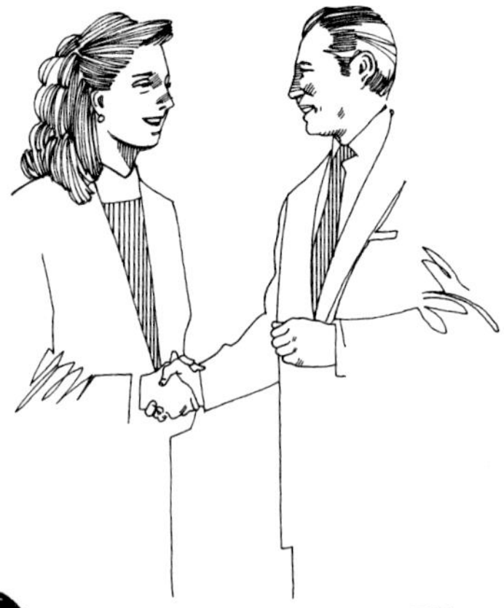

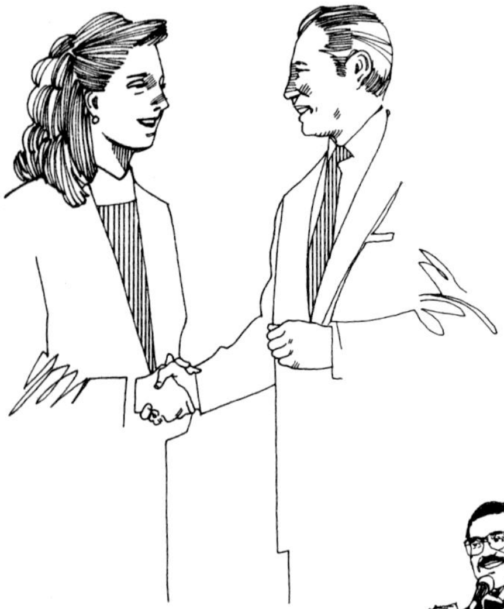

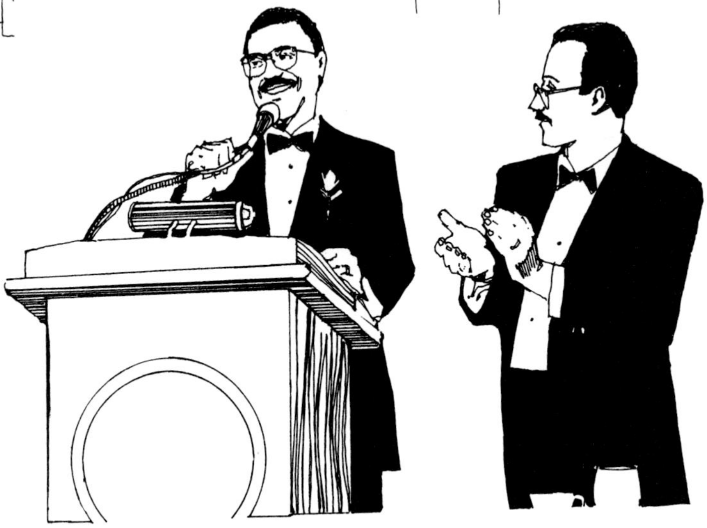

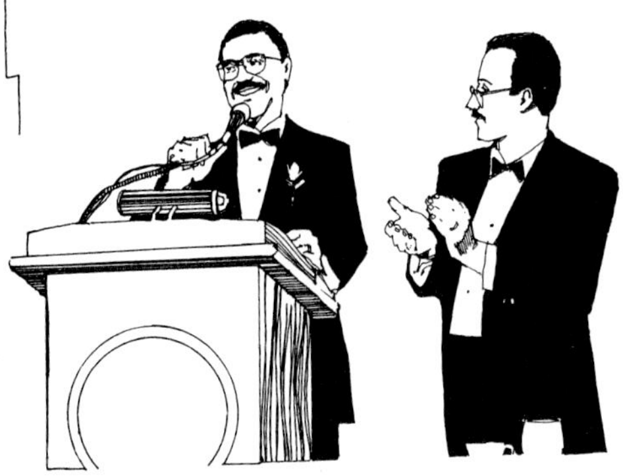

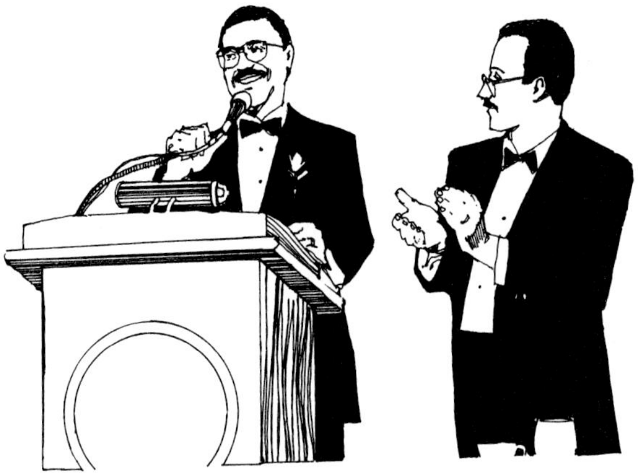

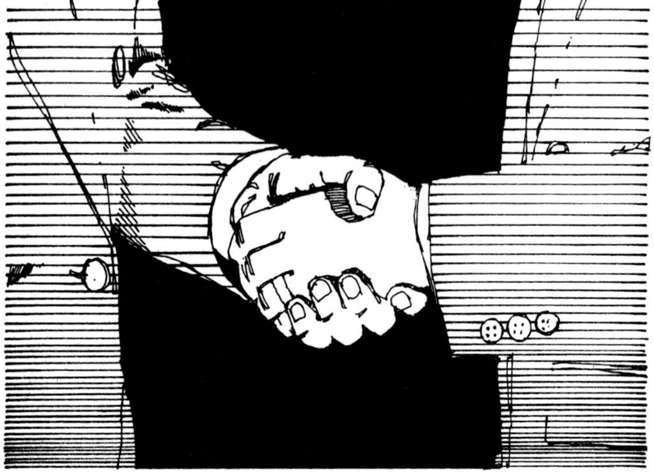

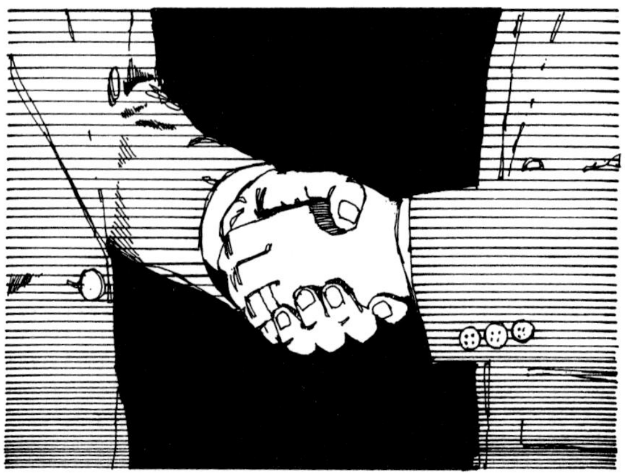

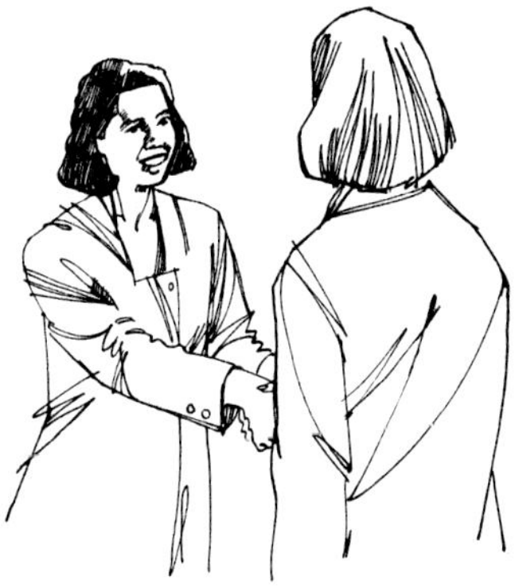
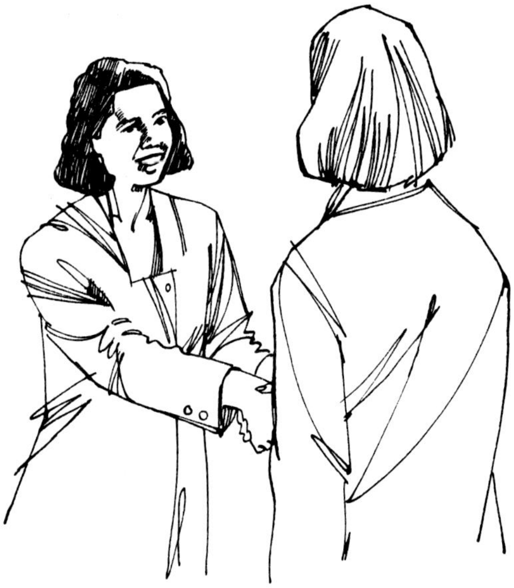
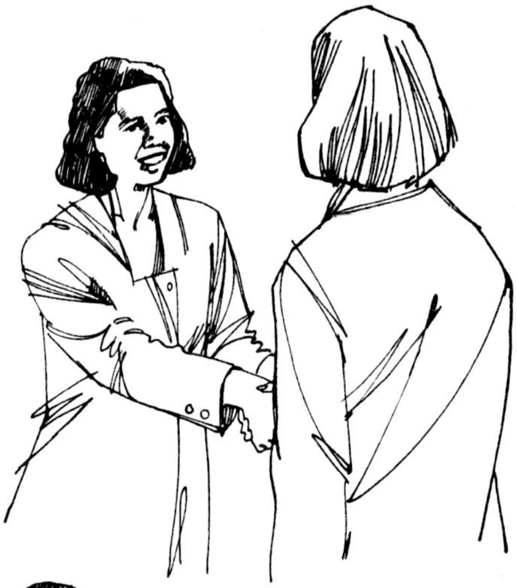
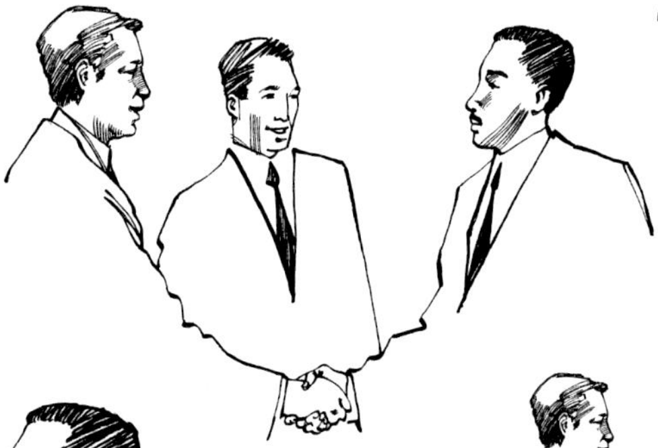
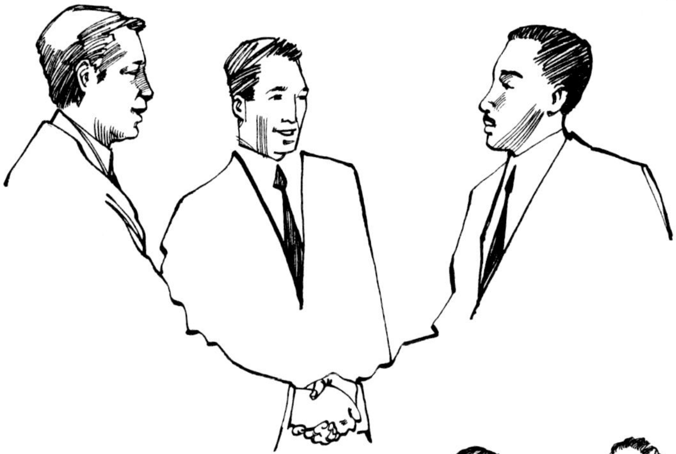
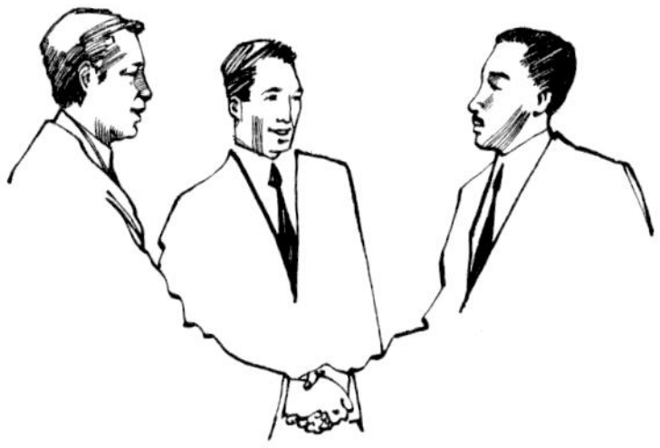
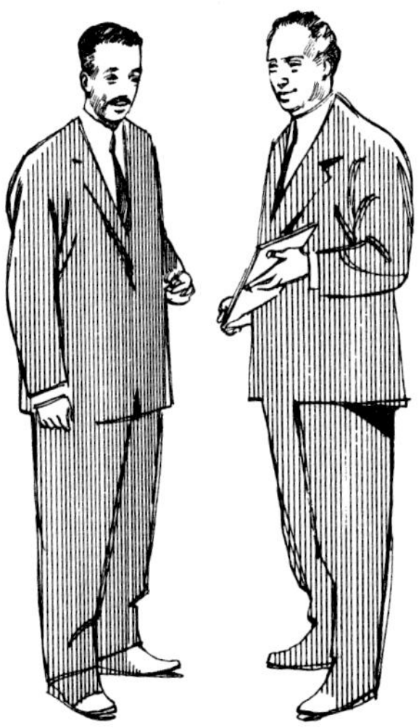
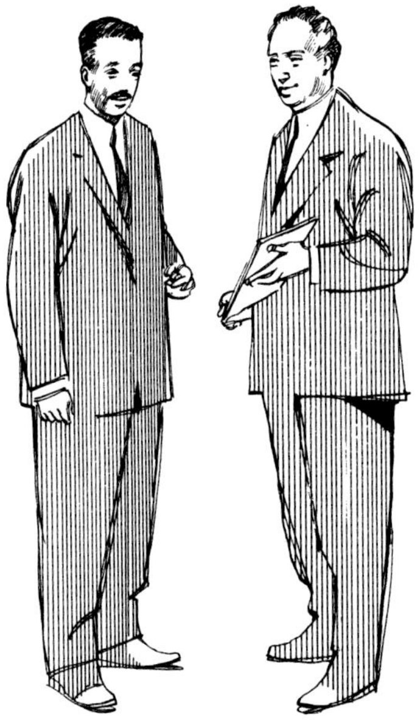
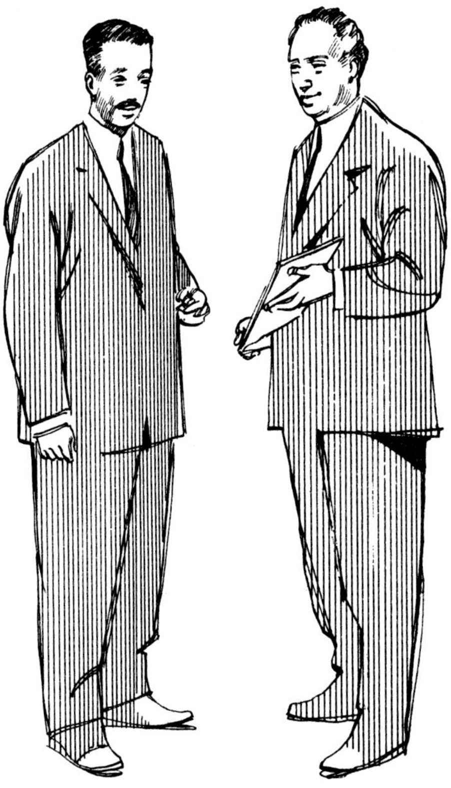

Balloons

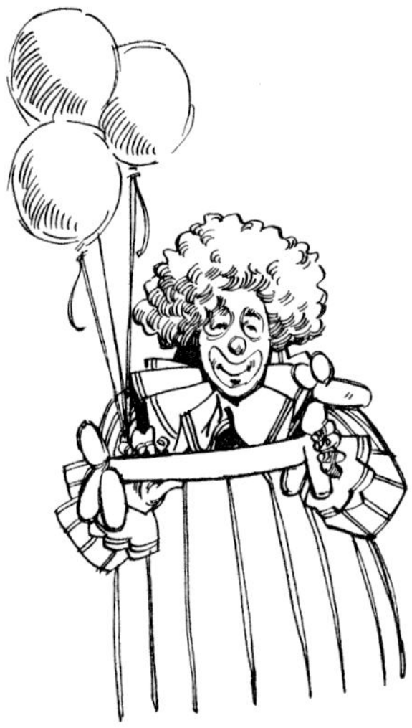

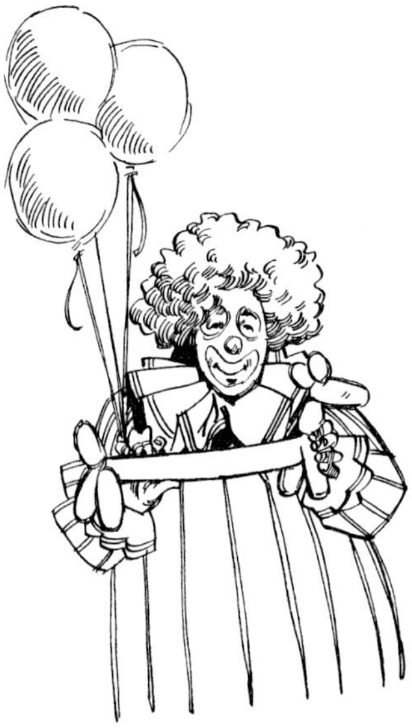

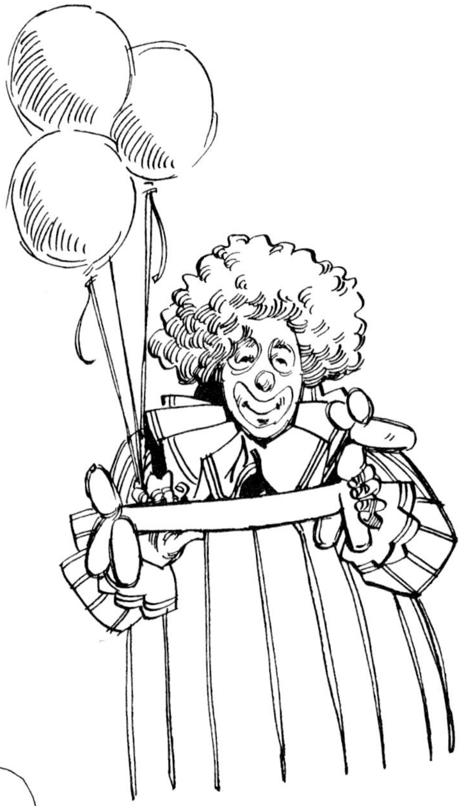

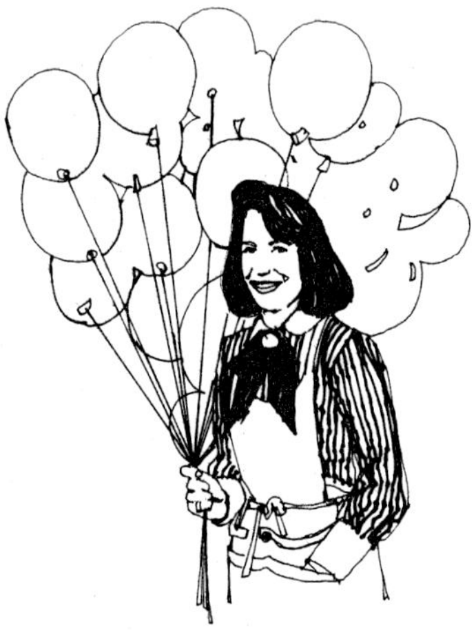

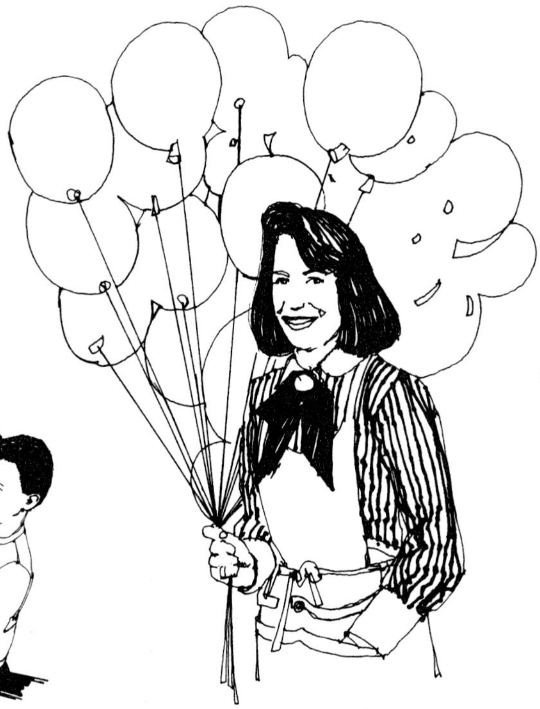

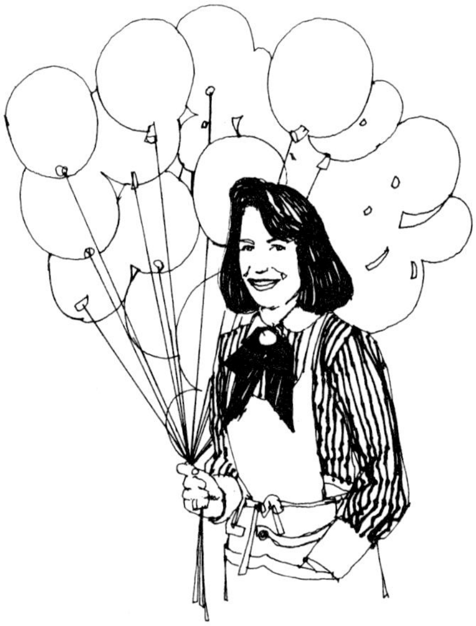

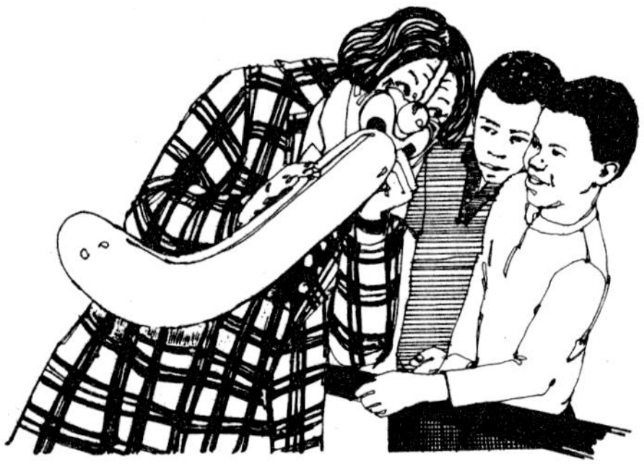

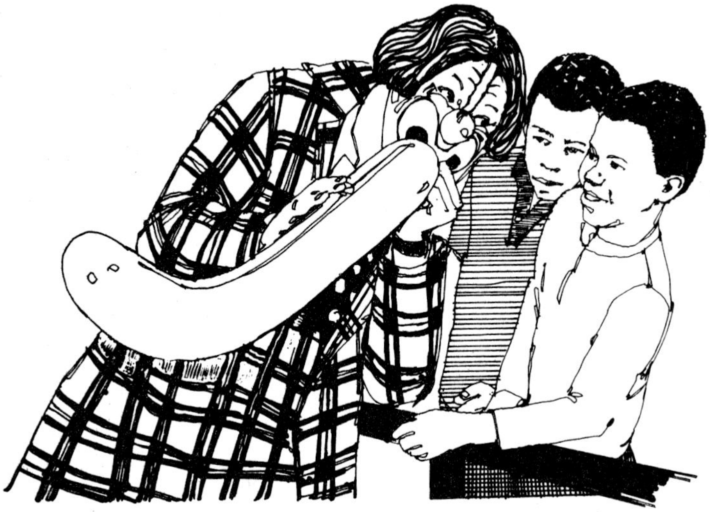

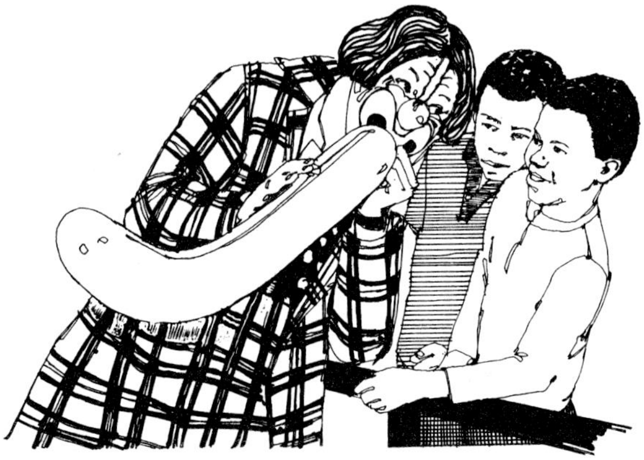

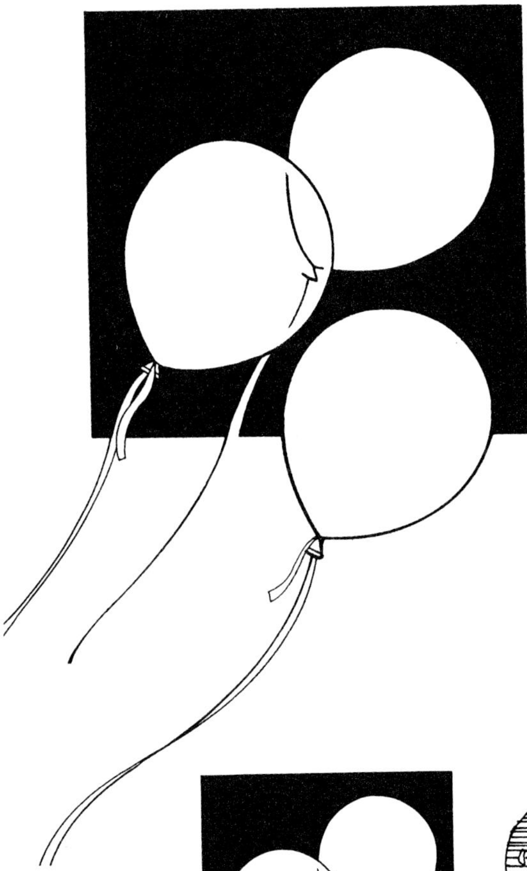

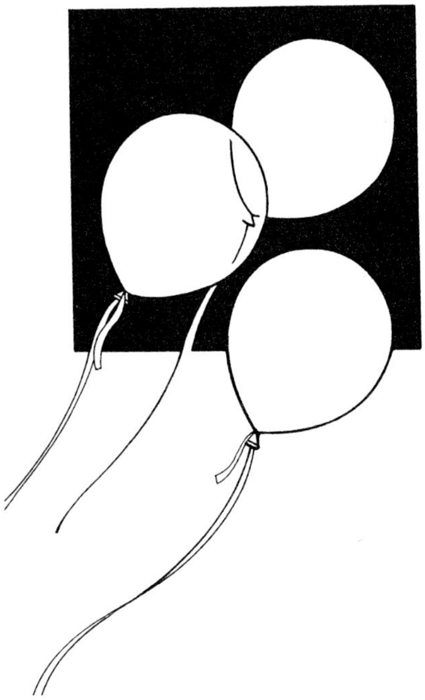

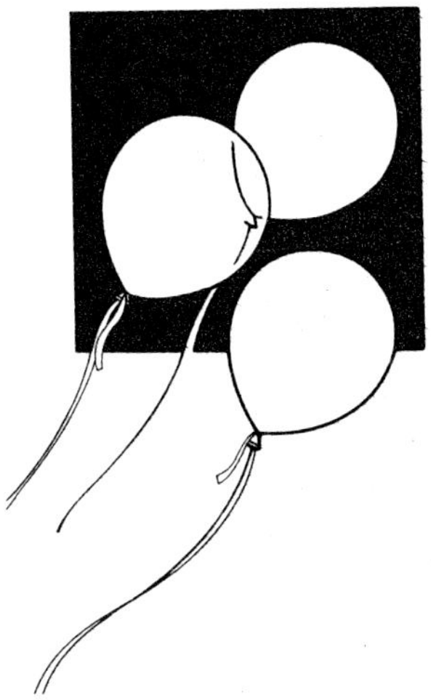

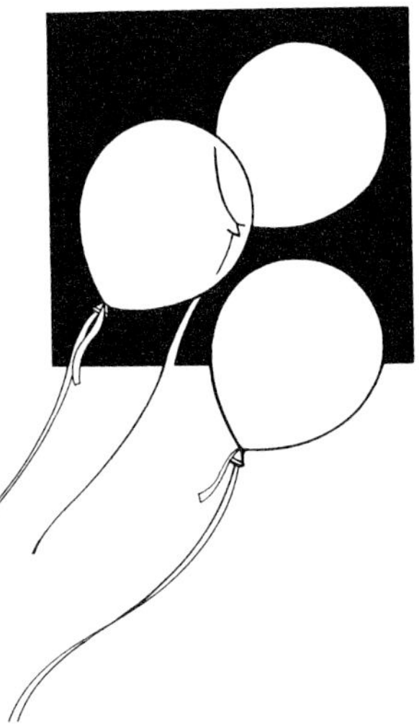

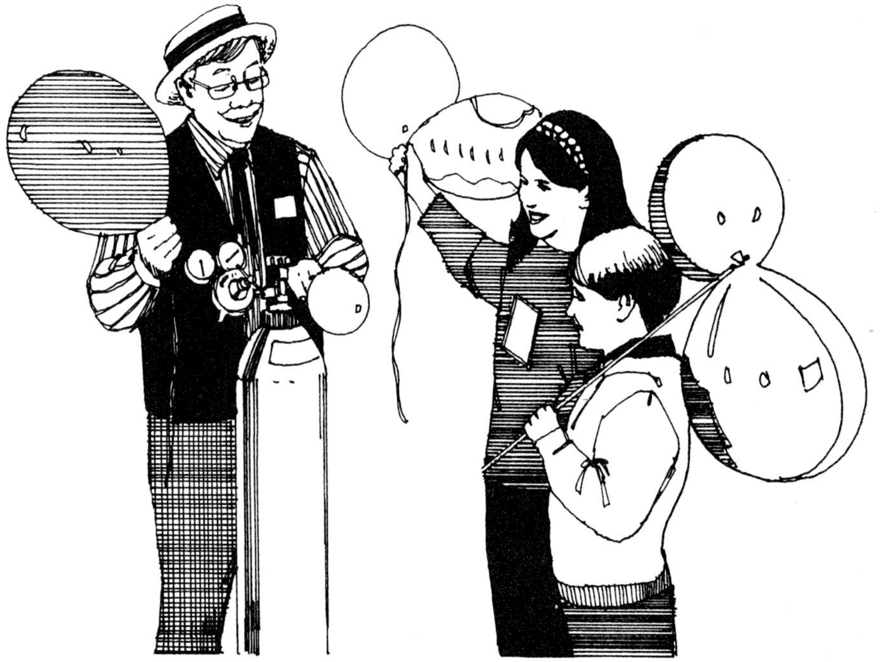

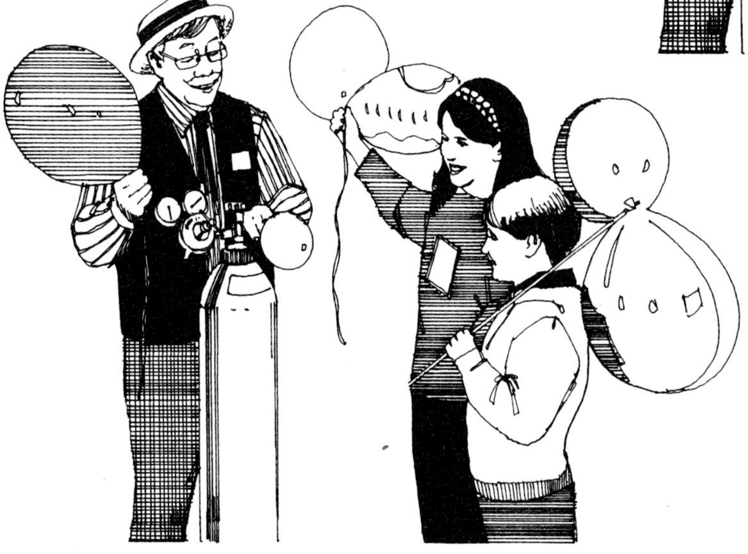

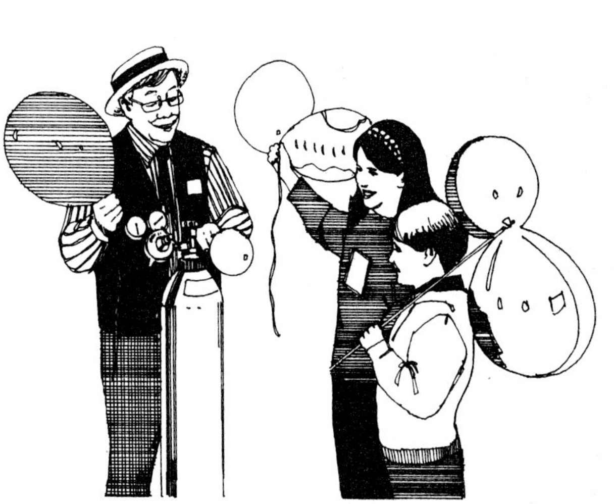

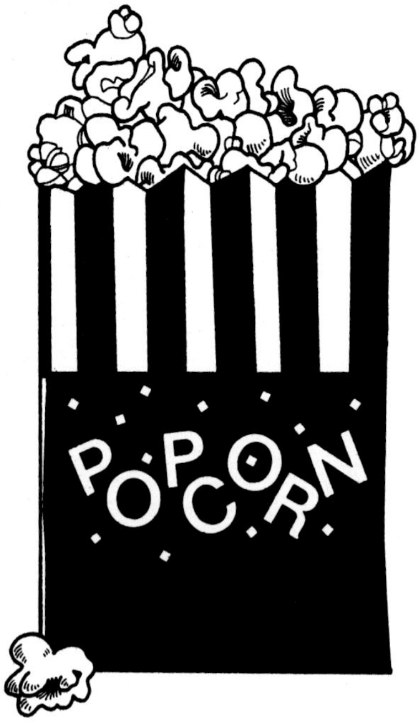
POPCORN

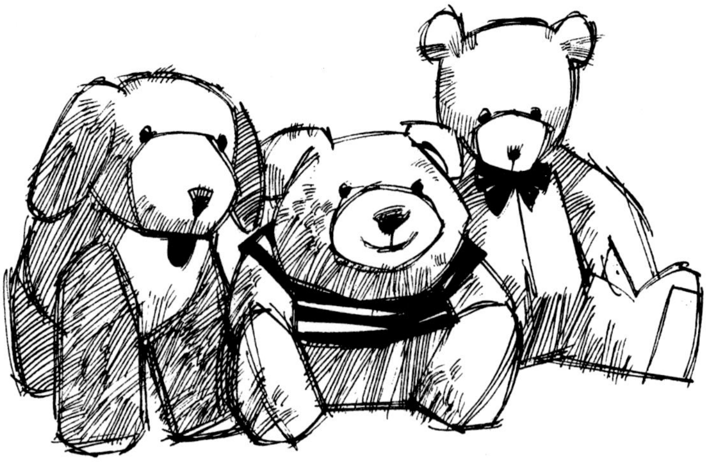

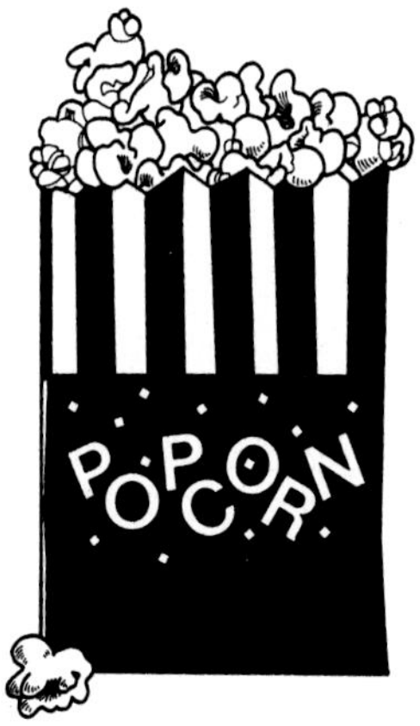
POPCORN

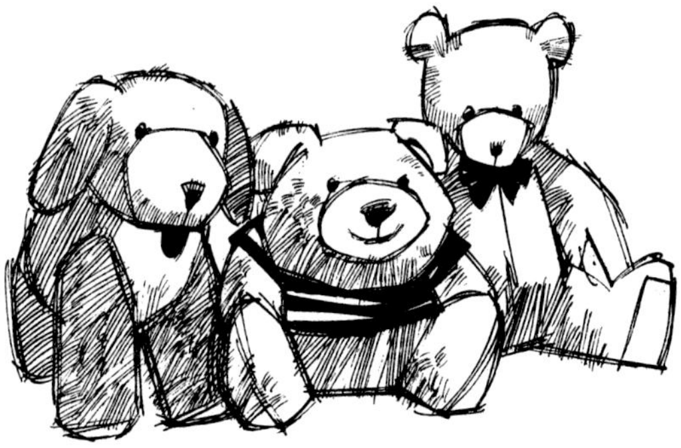

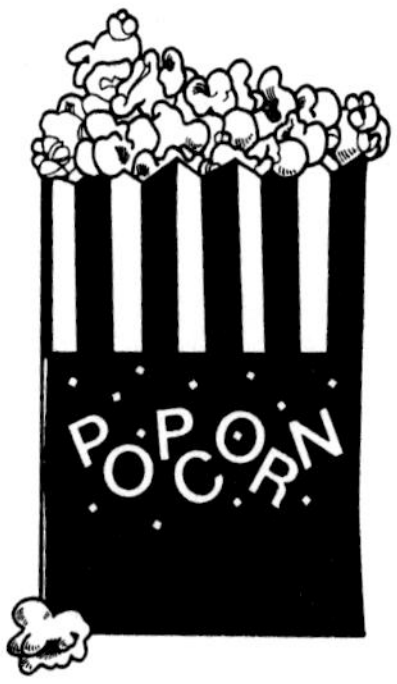
POPCORN

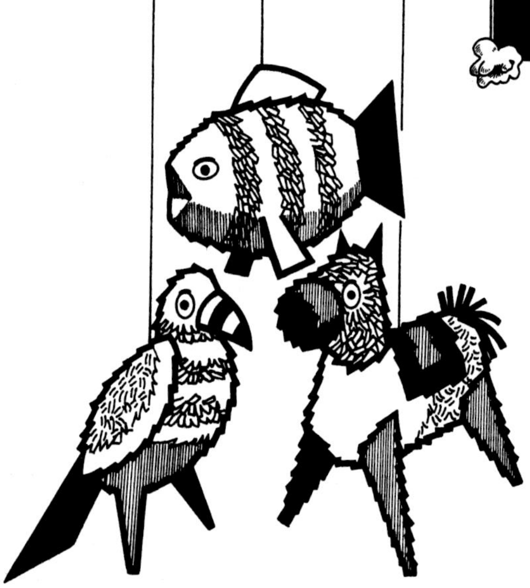

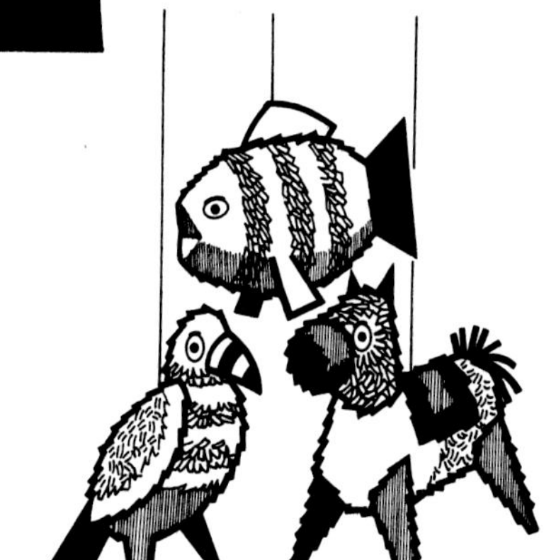

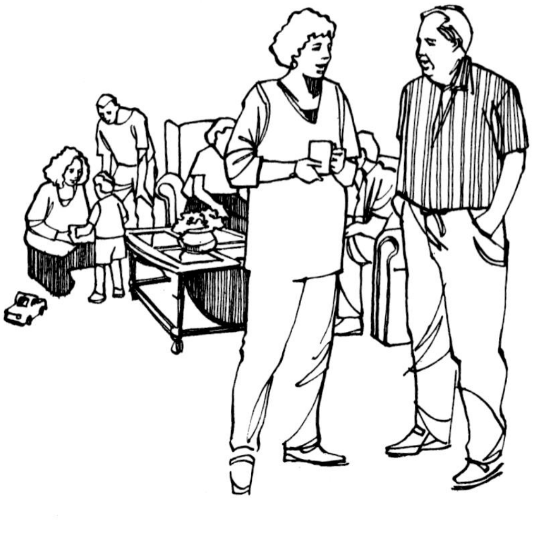

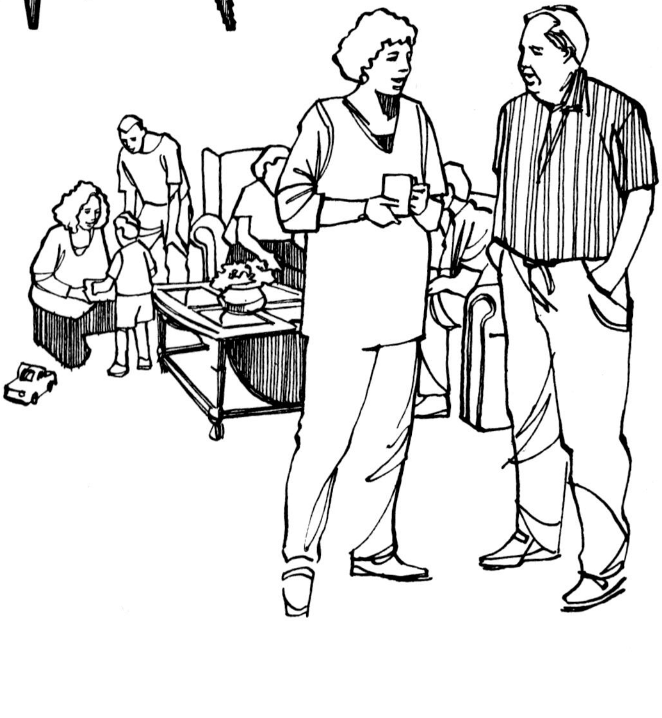

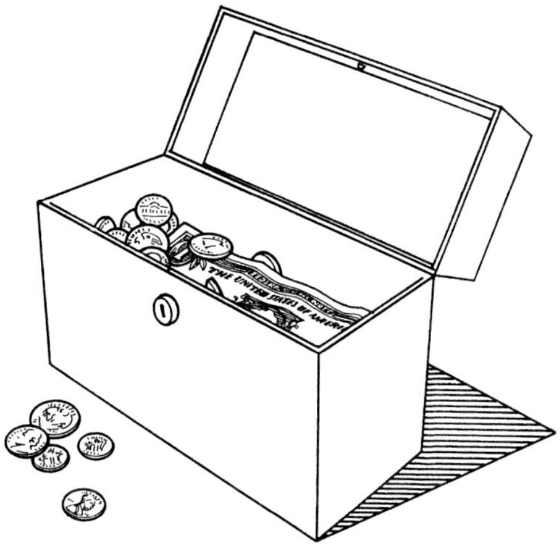

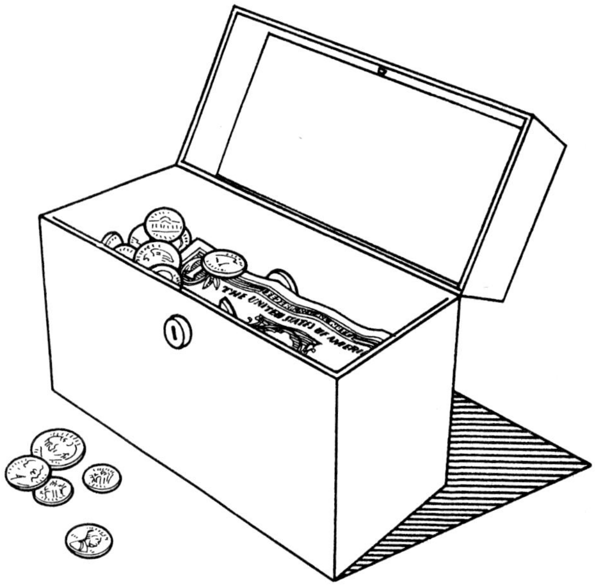

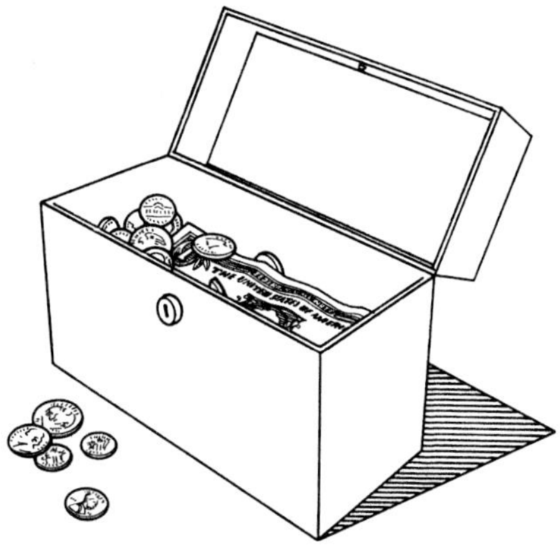

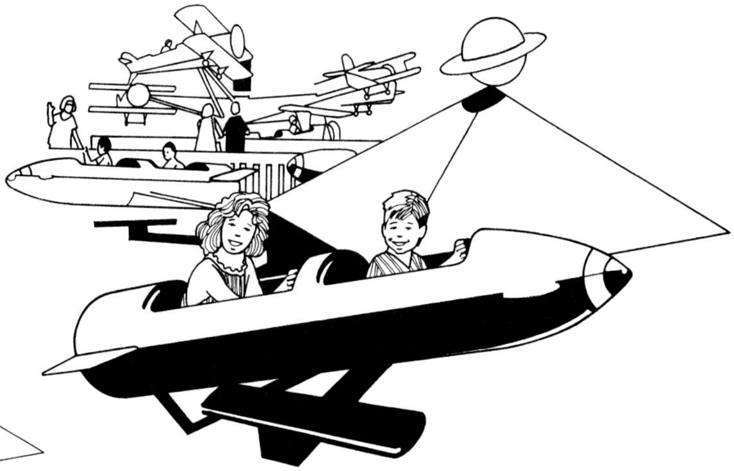

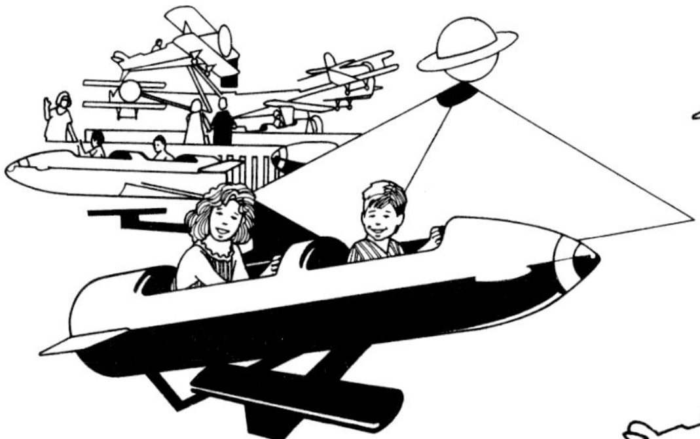

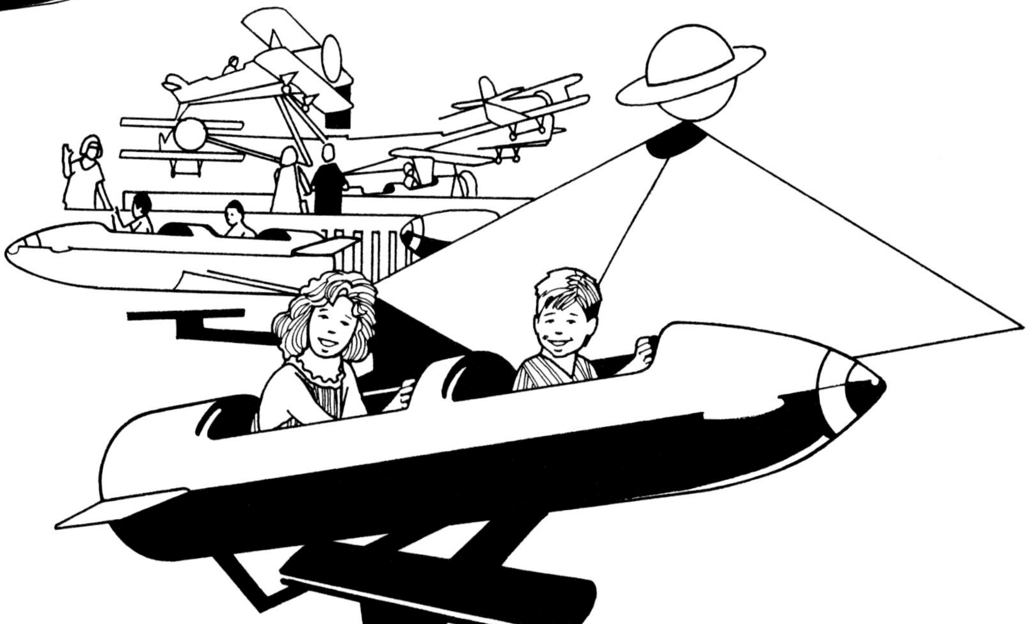

Miscellaneous

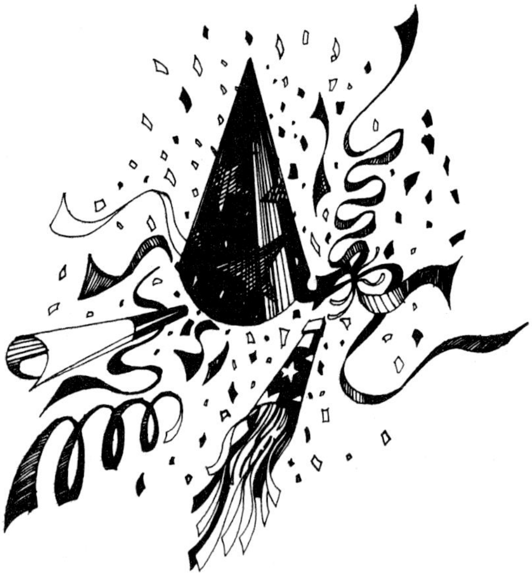

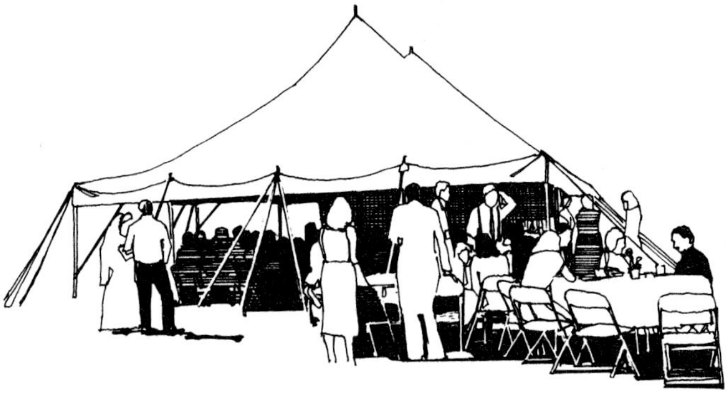

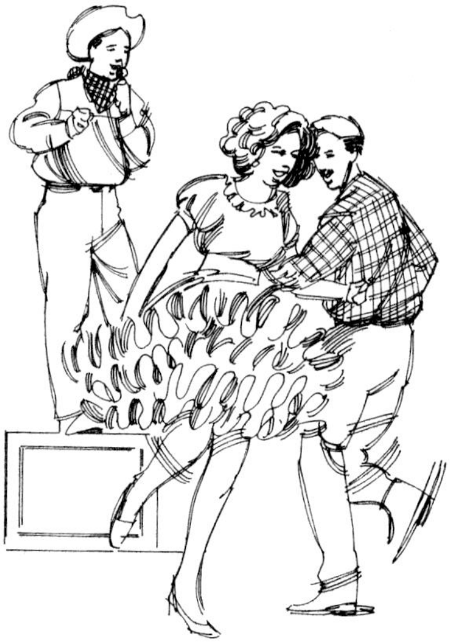

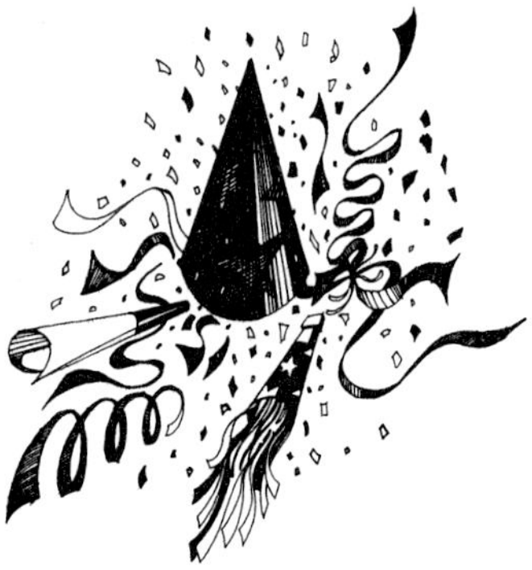

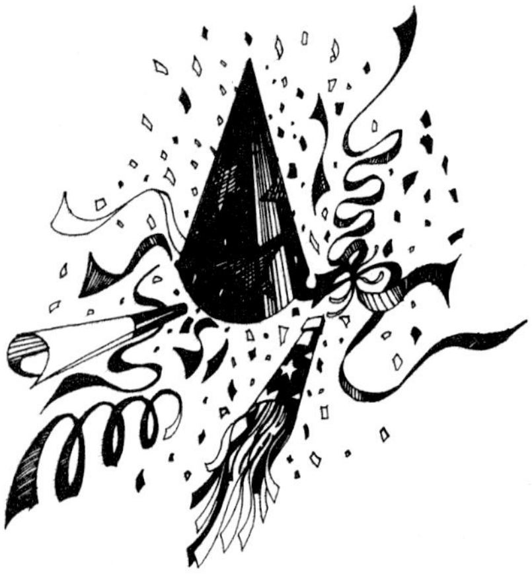

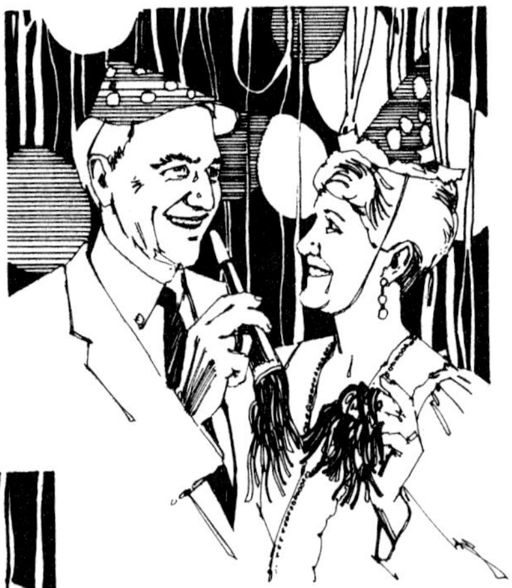

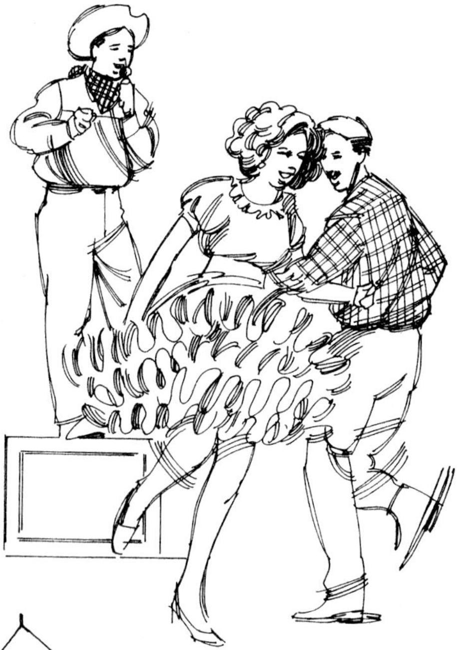

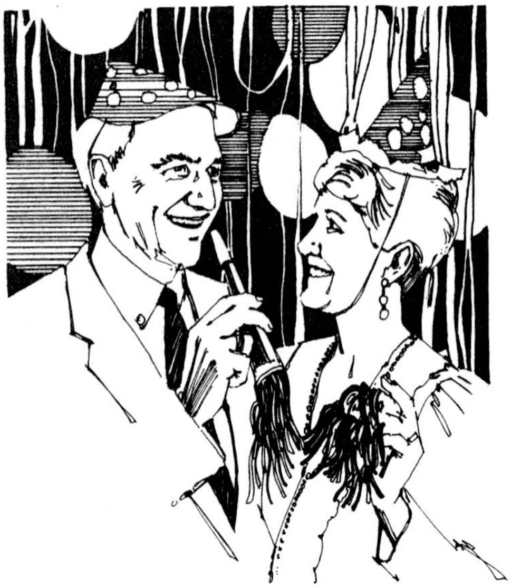

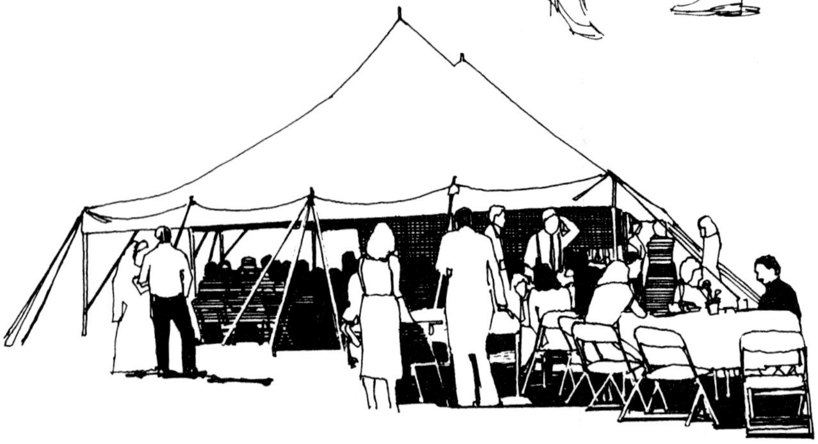